Nature Pictorialized

Nature Pictorialized

"THE VIEW" IN LANDSCAPE HISTORY

Gina Crandell

The Johns Hopkins University Press

BALTIMORE AND LONDON

Published in cooperation with the Center
for American Places, Harrisonburg, Virginia

The Johns Hopkins University Press
2715 North Charles Street
Baltimore, Maryland 21218-4319
The Johns Hopkins Press Ltd., London

Title-page illustration: Etching by Hearne and Pouncy from
Richard Payne Knight's *The Landscape* (1794). Reproduced by permission
of the Syndics of Cambridge University Library, Cambridge.

Library of Congress Cataloging-in-Publication Data

Crandell, Gina.
Nature pictorialized : "the view" in landscape history / Gina Crandell.
p.   cm.
Includes bibliographical references and index.
ISBN 0-8018-4397-9 (alk. paper)
1. Landscape architecture—History.   2. Landscape painting—Influence.
3. Landscape.   4. Nature (Aesthetics).   5. Landscape assessment.
6. Nature—Pictorial works.   I. Title.
SB4705.C73   1992
712'.2'09—dc20   92-7990

FOR LENA AND SHANA

Contents

Illustrations

Acknowledgments

I did not write this book alone. I would like to acknowledge and thank David Roochnik, who taught me how to express my ideas in writing, encouraged me to write, and faithfully edited this manuscript in its many versions over the years.

I am grateful to my professors at North Carolina State University, who taught me to question the basic tenets of my profession; and I thank Denis Wood, who recently commented on some of my writing. The Design Research Institute of the College of Design at Iowa State University funded my travel to Italy to see gardens and paintings. My colleagues here were helpful: Sidney Robinson piqued my interest in the picturesque, Al Rutledge provided the time for my work, and Jamie Horwitz and Mark Chidister provided supportive conversation.

I would also like to thank Kenneth Helphand at the University of Oregon, who served as the reader for the Johns Hopkins University Press; George F. Thompson, president of the Center for American Places and a publishing consultant to the Johns Hopkins University Press, who served as my editor; Miriam Kleiger, who copy-edited the manuscript; and those at the Johns Hopkins University Press who have worked on the publication of the book.

Nature Pictorialized

Introduction:
The Nature of Landscape

This book is born of perplexity and some frustration. As a professor of landscape architecture I am regularly confronted with the phrase "man and nature" to describe our relationship to the landscape we see. I find these words troubling, because they set up a dichotomy in which "man," because he is separate, can distance himself from "nature." With such distance men can then look at nature as an object. This may not sound problematic: what, after all, is wrong with looking at nature as an object outside ourselves? Perhaps nothing. I argue, however, that a particular way of looking has come to dominate and thus to distort our view of nature. In the eyes of many who value it, nature has come to be seen as a particular type of object, symbolized by a view that can be pictured.

This way of seeing, which I call "the pictorialization of nature," is the focus of this book. In powerful ways, pictures influence, and perhaps even help to constitute, our perception of places. For example, today pictures often first induce us to visit various places, and then encourage us to photograph these places when we get there. There is a specific set of pictures that, whether we have studied them or not, have helped to mold our conception of the landscape and have thereby played a crucial role in the objectification, or pictorialization, of nature: landscape paintings (and photographs of them). It is widely agreed that these pictures have had a great influence on the history of landscape architecture. While this is no doubt true, the significance of landscape paintings goes beyond their role in helping to shape various gardens. In the pages that follow, I argue that landscape paintings are an important source for the study of the history of seeing. They will help us to understand not only the very specific field of landscape architecture but also the very broad issue of the pictorialization of nature.

Man and Nature

With the phrase "man and nature," my colleagues and students believe they are making a very clear distinction. There is that which is made by man, and that which is "made" by nature (i.e., "the natural"). But in fact the distinction is not clear at all. The lack of clarity becomes evident when we test these terms. For example, we would not typically call the desert that has recently appeared in the Sahara "man-made," and yet this desertification is the result of human actions on dry and fragile ecosystems. In a parallel fashion, landscape architects often call some of their most contrived designs "natural" when, precisely because they are designs, they are not natural at all. Or consider the rose. Surely this famous flower is natural. But the morphology of the rose suggests that in an important sense it is quite "man-made." Its forms, colors, fragrance, and blooming cycles have been altered primarily to adjust it to changing notions of class and gender.[1] Furthermore, even if we can be sure of what is man-made, this phrase simply excludes the activity of all other creatures. "If ants had a language they would, no doubt, call their anthill an artifact and describe the brick wall in its neighbourhood as a *natural* object. *Nature* in fact would be for them all that was not 'ant-made.'"[2] In short, the tired old phrase "man and nature," which may, at times, seem perfectly clear, is anything but.

As its etymology suggests, *nature* (from the Latin *natura,* which itself is from *nasci,* to be born) refers to dynamic living processes and not to a static view. Strictly speaking, nature is not some particular thing we can point to, and it has no opposite. Nevertheless, there is a sense in which "nature" has regularly been seen as distinct from "man," and that is when it is personified as female.[3] Throughout the eighteenth century, "nature [was] variously described as a coy or seductive maiden, as a promiscuous or chaste consort, as a naked or overadorned damsel."[4] As recently as the nineteenth century, nature could be thought of as a companion for a solitary man, as when Thoreau said, "All nature is my bride."[5] For John Muir, the well-known conservationist, "the solitude of the wilderness is a sublime mistress, but an intolerable wife."[6] Men have envisioned nature as their sexual complement. The one, perhaps the only, thing that can be said in favor of this "nature-as-woman" concept is that it does not totally objectify nature: Thoreau's bride was not literally the forest; she was the spirit of the forest.

At about the same time that Thoreau was writing, George Perkins Marsh popularized the phrase "man and nature" with his book *Man and Nature,* written in 1864.[7] He specifically distinguished "man" from "nature" because he wanted to illuminate the damage men were doing to their environment. Today, possibly because of the conservation movement of which Marsh was a leader, "man" and "nature" have come to mean "people" and "environments that have not been too badly damaged." But is nature simply an undamaged environment? More importantly, how do we decide what nature is?

It is, of course, extremely difficult to define nature. The following is Kenneth Clark's attempt in his book *Landscape into Art:*

"Throughout this book, when I have used the word 'nature,' I have meant that part of the world not created by man which we can see with our unaided senses. Up to fifty years ago this anthropocentric definition did well enough. But since then the microscope and telescope have so greatly enlarged the range of our vision that the snug, sensible nature which we can see with our own eyes has ceased to satisfy our imaginations."[8]

Today we could supplement Clark's list of technological images with satellite photographs. More importantly, however, Clark's description raises a basic question: is nature something we can see, either with our eyes or with our technological devices? Is nature something to be seen at all? With or without our devices, what we call nature is really just a snapshot of the surface of complex, ongoing processes.

We are not only anthropocentric but also fatally arrogant if we believe that nature is something we can point to from a car window and distinguish from that which has been created by man. It is precisely this visual, or pictorial, conception of nature that typically dominates the use of the word today. It is as if we believe we can point to anything green and growing that has not been damaged recently, and pronounce it natural.

One consequence of this type of thinking is that we have fenced off a few "enclaves of nature" for picnics and day hikes. Nature has been relegated to a small and distant, refreshing but finally unimportant, part of our lives. We want desperately to think of forested mountains or craggy river valleys, or even their second-hand imitations designed for parks in cities, as nature itself. And so we call Central Park, which was once a marsh but in 1860 was made into wooded hills and curving lakes by Frederick Law Olmsted and Calvert Vaux, "natural."

We have framed nature by fencing off what we take to be its best examples. We have chosen to preserve the geysers of Yellowstone and have forced the marsh in Manhattan to be covered with something more "natural." But how did we determine what the best examples of nature are? In what way is a geyser superior to a marsh? I suggest that there is one answer to these questions: we have defined and judged nature on the basis of its conformity with pictures. That which is most deserving of protection is that which is most beautiful. In turn, as I shall argue, "beautiful" has really meant "most pictorially satisfying."

Thomas Moran was an unrivaled painter of the beauty of wilderness. He participated in the 1871 Yellowstone expedition, and subsequently his art assisted the campaign for the establishment of the first national park. When Congress in 1874 appropriated ten thousand dollars for one of Moran's paintings of the Grand Canyon to hang in the Senate lobby, some of the continent's wildest territory had received official endorsement as a subject for national pride and preservation. Above all, nature had been pictorialized, and the Grand Canyon would be remembered as Thomas Moran had learned to picture it.[9]

To us, the beauty of wild places such as the Grand Canyon seems obvious. But people in earlier times have not always perceived this beauty. For example, consider a scene that today we automatically think of as beautiful: a distant view of an Alpine mountain. For hundreds of years, such mountains were thought of as threatening and unappealing. It was only late in the sixteenth century that opinions changed. What is most striking about this change is that it was caused by the spread of pictorial images of mountains. "The discovery of Alpine scenery does not precede but follows the spread of prints and paintings with mountain panoramas."[10] Pictures influence behavior and perception, and we have learned to appreciate the beauty of actual mountains by first seeing pictures of them.

It was a fateful moment in the history of seeing when mountains were pictorialized, as it was when much later a representation of the Grand Canyon was placed on a wall. For at that moment Americans began to see themselves as detached and privileged spectators, even collectors, of nature's beauty. Over the years this habit has become firmly entrenched, and nature, once the most powerful of forces, became framed and pictorialized.

We realize, of course, that nature is not simply a representation in a frame, or a place to hike on weekends. But our language and our actions suggest that this is precisely what it is. We should understand that nature is not simply an object we can point to, paint, and photograph. In fact, the "nature" we look at and point to is always a landscape and not nature itself.

Landscape

The conflation of the words *landscape* and *nature* is more than a simple problem of semantics; instead, it raises an issue of fundamental importance, for this error is a consequence of the man/nature dichotomy. Human beings believe they are separate from nature, which they view as an object, more specifically, a pictorial object. This means that what we think of as nature has been mediated by pictorial activities such as appropriation, framing, and re-presenting. In a parallel fashion, the landscape has been designed by human beings. To think it is not, to think that a landscape is natural, is thus to perpetuate the fundamental error of pictorializing nature.

J. B. Jackson's definition of *landscape* makes this point clear: *"A landscape is thus a space deliberately created to speed up or slow down the process of nature."*[11] A landscape is thus analogous to a domesticated animal. Both involve the manipulation of an otherwise natural life cycle. The well-bred horse is kept in a "youthful" state by feeding, as is the park, by mowing. It is as difficult today to find wild horses as it is to find a place that is truly natural—a place where natural processes have not been speeded up or slowed down by some kind of modification.

Plowing, harvesting, building, excavating, and planting are all examples of cultural intrusions, but many cultural intrusions are more subtle. What about photographing? Does taking a picture deep in the Brazilian rain forest constitute modification of the forest? I suspect it might. If it is not modification in the literal sense, it probably means that tourists or business interests are not far away. Does the fact that satellites have photographed every part of the world therefore mean that the earth itself is now "landscape"? I think so. Does such widespread intrusion therefore suggest that we control nature? Certainly not.

While landscape is something that we can see in photographs or point to from car windows, it should be remembered that it has not always been thought of as a view. Seeing the landscape is not simply retinal; it is based on a very long history. The word *land* has origins in agriculture. "As far back as we can trace the word, 'land' meant a defined space, one with *boundaries,* though not necessarily one with fences or walls. The word has so many derivative meanings that it rivals in ambiguity the word 'landscape.' Three centuries ago it was still being used in everyday speech to signify a fraction of plowed ground no larger than a quarter acre, then to signify an expanse of village holdings, as in grassland or woodland, and then finally to signify England itself—the largest space any Englishman of those days could imagine; in short, a remarkably versatile word, but always implying a space defined by people, and one that could be described in legal terms."[12]

We all make boundaries. Farmers make fence lines. Street vendors define spaces under their Cinzano umbrellas. Homeowners identify their property with border privet. Political boundaries have now been placed over the entire world, thus supporting the proposition that the entire surface of the earth is now landscape, that is, modified by boundaries. Obviously, most of the boundaries out there were not made by environmental designers. It is important to recognize, however, that creating boundaries is precisely what designers principally do.

Architects delineate boundaries with walls and changes in construction materials; artists distinguish between what is and what isn't. Landscape architects construct (or conceal) boundaries with vegetation, landforms, walls, and paving. But there is one great pretense that characterizes landscape architects—we try to disguise the fact that we are actually making boundaries. We do this by calling our designs "natural." To title a book *Natural Landscaping,* for example, is not only to use an oxymoron but also to suggest that when we create boundaries and speed up or slow down the processes of nature we need not admit what we are doing. Indeed, landscape architects speed up processes in some spots by introducing plants and slow them down in adjacent spots with paving. The landscape represents deliberate change. It is a cumulative product of everyone's boundaries.

"No group sets out to create a landscape, of course. What it sets out to do is to create a community, and the landscape as its visible manifestation is simply the by-product of people working and living, sometimes coming together, sometimes staying apart, but always recognizing their interdependence."[13] To think of the landscape as natural, if naturalness implies being untouched by human beings, flies in the face of its history.

The View

The process by which the landscape has been given boundaries has been neither isolated nor an accidental one. Instead, it has proceeded in tandem with the development of a set of artistic conventions. These, in turn, have largely been derived from pictorial sources. "There is no word in English which denotes a tract of land, of whatever extent, which is apprehended visually, but not, necessarily, pictorially. . . . we can speak of the 'landscape' of a country, but in doing so we introduce, whether we want to or not, notions of value and form which relate, not just to seeing the land, but to seeing it in a certain way—pictorially."[14]

We each have a mental picture of nature. It probably includes trees and grass, and maybe a river or mountains that we see from a distance. More importantly, we ascribe a kind of innocence to it, thinking of it as pretty and benign. Where did such a picture come from? As we shall see below, one of the primary sources of our way of seeing the landscape is the long series of developments in painting which can be called naturalism.[15] The history of naturalistic painting chronicles the development of conventions that created convincing illusions of views to the world outside.

Today we believe that, and speak as if, our seeing has no history. We assume, for example, that representing a landscape from a single viewer's location is a timeless or natural way of looking at and picturing the world. But this is not so. Such representations, whether paintings or photographs, use a very specific convention, namely the linear perspective developed during the Renaissance. In the landscape illustration of the Western world, for example, some two thousand years passed before the view based on the spectator's location became a standard convention for picturing places.

E. H. Gombrich offers a good example of a pictorial convention and a method of painting quite different from the linear perspective to which we are accustomed. His example is an Egyptian painting of a pond (fig. 1.1). To us this picture looks like a very strange assortment of views; they could never be seen from a single location. Each feature is depicted in its most characteristic shape, the one that gives us the most information. The Egyptian artists "drew from memory, according to strict rules which ensured that everything that had to go into the picture would stand out in perfect clarity. Their method, in fact, resembled that of the map-maker rather than that of the painter. . . . They would simply draw the pond as if it were seen from above,

Fig. 1.1. *Wall Painting of a Pond* (about 1400 B.C.E.), from a tomb in Thebes. Reproduced by courtesy of the Trustees of the British Museum, London.

and the trees from the side. The fishes and birds in the pond, on the other hand, would hardly look recognizable as seen from above, so they were drawn in profile."[16] Thus to the ancient Egyptians it would have been only natural to expect that a picture of a place would be depicted not from a singular point of view, but in such a way as to reveal the most information about each of the objects depicted. (This is a technique that today might well be useful in site analysis.)

The point of view from which we look at, organize, and evaluate the landscape today is dependent on a specific pictorial convention developed in the fifteenth century. Linear perspective creates the illusion of seeing spatial relationships from a single vantage point. It glorifies the spectator by organizing everything in the picture in relation to the location of the eye of the beholder. It takes absolute control of the subject and submits it as an object for view. Such an attitude, as the contrast cited above clearly indicates, is culturally conditioned; it is historically determined and not natural at all.

The Landscape Garden

What happens when a view that we take to be innocent, but that in fact is not, motivates our designs? There is no doubt that the eighteenth-century English landscape garden has been the most influential force in the last two centuries of landscape design. The crucial theme of this book is that this garden was itself based on pictorial conventions borrowed from naturalistic painting. As a result, when a landscape architect imitates an English garden by putting a serpentine lake in front of a corporate headquarters, and then describes the resulting effect as natural, he or she is quite mistaken.[17]

The "landscape" garden tried to disguise its boundaries and to conceal the fact that it was designed. It pretended it had followed nature's temporal rhythms when it had not. The pretense was all too successful. Today when we think of nature we too often conjure up images borrowed from eighteenth-century England. This is an extraordinary fact that we rarely question. Consider the ubiquitous lawn that surrounds so many houses in the United States. Why mown grass? Why clumps of shrubs? Because we want some "nature" to look at from our windows. This vision is so powerful that grass is even planted in the arid landscape of suburban Arizona. But why is this grass taken to be any more natural than the desert plants that predated the founding of Phoenix? Because we have become enthralled by the vision of eighteenth-century England. We do not think of tropical or desert landscapes, for example, when we try to visualize "nature." Instead, we see rolling hills, deep green masses of trees, serpentine lakes, and cleanly shaven lawns. Perhaps all this was appropriate for England: the sheep had to eat something. But it makes no sense in Phoenix or Las Vegas. The goal of this book is to deconstruct the landscape garden's disguise: neither the English landscape garden nor its many progeny are natural. They are products of a very specific cultural tradition, namely, that of naturalistic painting.

Again, the word *landscape* is itself instructive here. When it entered the English language at the beginning of the seventeenth century, *landscape* did not refer to what one saw outdoors—it was a painter's word introduced to describe sixteenth-century Dutch paintings. It was, according to the *Oxford English Dictionary (OED),* "a picture representing natural inland scenery, as distinguished from a sea picture, portrait, etc."[18]

It was not until more than a century later, according to the *OED,* that Alexander Pope would use the word *landscape* in his 1725 translation of the *Odyssey* to refer to a view or prospect such as can be seen at a glance from a fixed point of view. And although Pope may here mean a view of an actual landscape and not just a picture, his definition of *landscape* is still restricted, as a picture is, to that which can be taken in by a spectator's glance. Obviously, a prospect or view takes its meaning from pictures even when it transfers the view to actual landscapes. The purpose of this book is to follow the representation of landscape in paintings until the concept of the landscape makes its break with the canvas and is transferred to actual landscapes.

It is well known that the seventeenth-century landscape paintings that had been imported to England from Italy were the predominant influence on English taste in landscape.[19] These paintings certainly did not document actual places, nor did they attempt to disguise cultural modifications. Instead, they were attempts to create a certain mood and to portray subjects from classical literature. Such paintings were based on conventions for depicting landscape and on compositional techniques intended to make works of art more satisfying than actual places. Imagined and ideal landscapes represented a nature perfected and composed by men painting in studios.

The crucial point, however, is that the eighteenth-century *landscape* garden—which, to reiterate, is widely acknowledged to be the most influential force in the last two centuries of landscape design—was itself based on pictorial conventions borrowed from these paintings. This is the classic example of the power pictures have had, not only as sources of landscape design but also as a force that shaped our conception of a composed and ideal nature.

When a painting is called naturalistic, which is a description I will use for most landscape paintings, it means that artists have employed convincing pictorial conventions to create the illusion of something a spectator might see. No one thinks that the painting was not made by human hands or that it must be a realistic depiction of an actual place. But when a landscape design is called natural, as is the English landscape garden even today, this designation cuts it off from its cultural roots even though it was originally designed to create an illusion, much like a naturalistic painting.

A fundamental inversion thus took place in the eighteenth century. For the first time in history a garden, or a designed landscape, had exchanged places with "nature." Before this century, unmodified land, such as wilderness or swamp, had surrounded carefully maintained gardens and agricultural landscapes. But in eighteenth-century England swamps were drained for agricultural expansion, and forests were planted in gardens. Landscape gardens, representing nature, had become enclaves surrounded by maintained landscapes. These gardens were modeled not after the swamps and wilderness that had once surrounded villages but after the techniques of painting that had been devised to create illusions of "nature." Indeed, both the land inside gardens and the land outside them were now landscapes, designed for quite different purposes.

The eighteenth-century English were not fooled into thinking that their landscape gardens were nature in a literal sense. After all, they had seen the destruction of the landscape that had existed before their gardens. Indeed, they had commissioned that it be reconstructed to look like the paintings they admired so much. Moreover, they had read the classical literature to which the allusions in the paintings referred. Today's environmental designers lack this knowledge and so have convinced themselves that what they see in the contemporary version of the landscape garden is "natural"; and today this description means almost nothing at all.

———

It is too often the case that the history of gardens is seen as the history of landscape architecture. However, as I have just suggested, these two histories are not equivalent, for painting is one of the great influences on the landscape. Indeed, the portrayal of landscape in paintings is one of the best records of how the "discovery of the landscape" (and, not incidentally, the development of gardens) unfolded. Clearly, the basic source material used in the history of landscape architecture and environmental design should take this fact into account. This book is not a comprehensive art historical text. Thus it does not concentrate on the basic issue treated by art historians when they discuss the relationship between landscape painting and nature—namely, how the paintings "[record] the effect of light."[20] Instead, this book takes its bearings from the essential project of the landscape architect, which is to alter an existing environment by imposing three-dimensional forms upon it. A landscape architect's dialogue with nature is based on the fact that the environment never ceases to change and always provides an inescapable context for everything he or she does. Too often the pictorial conventions of naturalism and the pastoral ideal have enthralled the landscape architect and overruled context. The consequence has been the perpetuation of an image of nature as green, beautiful, static, and benign. The pictorial conception of nature has not only failed to develop an authentic sensitivity to context but also helped to repress examination of its own history. Knowledge of that history can provide the foundation for understanding the pictorialization of nature, as well as the impetus for a revised representation of nature. Finally, it can even ignite an investigation into contemporary art and the role it might play in helping us view the landscape in new, and perhaps nonpictorial, ways.

Pictures

There are many illustrations in this book. This is typical of books about the landscape. Many of us learn about art, architecture, and landscape architecture via photographic reproductions. We do this unhesitatingly and, often, unquestioningly. Consequently, we need to think more carefully about making and using such pictures. We take our pictures to be what they seem obviously to be: representations of the world. However, when we do so, something far less obvious occurs: we take the world to be a picture.

We must understand, and keep in mind, that sight itself is affected by pictures. It is not simply a matter of making representations of what we see or propose to see. The very representations themselves actually affect what we see or propose. Even photographs, which we want to believe are accurate representations, are not the same as the world we see and therefore have the potential to modify what we see.

A painting provides a good example. Driving across the Iowa countryside on a lush summer day, I can see the topography and vegetation take on the bulbous and fertile forms of a Grant Wood painting. It is impossible to know what Grant Wood's experience of the Iowa landscape was, but there is no question that my own experience is changed, and heightened, by my having seen his paintings. Likewise, an iris can never again be ordinary to a viewer who has seen one painted by Georgia O'Keeffe.

Today most of us depend on pictures for much of our knowledge about the world. Landscape architects, whose very education is primarily based on pictures, are even more dependent. Design students' impressions of important landmarks from all over the world come from images projected in dark classrooms. All of these representations affect what we see when we actually see the real thing, and they affect what we imagine when we have never seen the original.

Drawing has always been considered a basic design skill, a way of filtering impressions and illustrating proposals. Drawing is based on pictorial conventions. We draw what we imagine on the basis of what we have seen, often in pictures. We shadow trees not because we walk around noticing trees with shadows, but because we have learned that shadows are a convention for showing three dimensions. "With few exceptions, cast shadows do not appear in painting until the Quattrocento [fifteenth century], yet we can hardly imagine that Trecento painters were unaware of shadows."[21] Depicting shadows is a convention learned from pictures. Since seeing itself is informed by pictorial conventions, we might consciously notice shadows under trees for the first time after we have drawn them or seen them in pictures.

Technical devices can also supplement our sight. A good example is the camera itself. It is a machine, a product of early nineteenth-century technological advances in methods of recording light. The camera was preceded by the camera obscura, a box that organized the world toward one small opening. Viewers could, after closing one eye, feel the excitement of having the world outside converge upon them. Although the camera obscura was known as far back as the late Middle Ages, it was not designed for viewing landscapes until late in the seventeenth century. Why would this be so? The reason is that the interest in viewing landscapes did not develop until *after* the growth in popularity of landscape paintings. Therefore, while technological devices can enlarge our vision, they do not do so until we express new interests. Once again, then, pictures have proven to be crucial in developing our interest in the landscape.

This genealogy of the camera suggests that the pictures we take for granted do not express natural ways of seeing the world. Instead, they are the results of a long series of cultural developments and *learned* perceptions. Furthermore, if we base our conception of nature on these very same pictures, as I think we often do, we are mistakenly calling "nature" what should really be called "landscape." And when we refer to what we see as landscape, we should recognize the cultural bases of both its construction and our conception of it.

A final example may help to punctuate this idea: consider the following anecdote, first written in Edward Norgate's *Miniatura* in 1650, and cited by Gombrich.[22] An adventurer and lover of art finds a painter working at his easel and recounts to him the adventures of a long journey—the cities he beheld, the beautiful prospects, Alpine rocks, and old castles. By the time the adventurer has ended his long discourse the painter, to the adventurer's astonishment, has recreated those places and that country, as if the painter had been on the journey. Knowing, as we do, to what extent landscape painters depend on convention rather than on the representation of actual places, we may not be totally surprised by this.

What should astonish us, however, is what motivated the adventurer to go in search of landscape prospects in the first place: it was the paintings the adventurer had seen. During frequent visits to the painter's house, the adventurer's understanding of "beauty spots" had been conditioned by the images he had seen in his friend's paintings. Gombrich concludes that "the idea of natural beauty as an inspiration for art . . . is, to say the least, a dangerous over-simplification. Perhaps it even reverses the actual process by which man discovers the beauty of nature."[23] We call the landscape beautiful if it reminds us of paintings we have seen.

Artists did not even go outside to make landscape paintings until the invention of tubes to hold oil paints in the nineteenth century. Before that time, although they may have sketched their observations of particular objects, the views they painted were, for the most part, based on compositional conventions they had learned from earlier pictures, and their paintings were produced in studios. We might assume that the invention of the oil paint tube was predicated on the desire to paint outdoors. Even further, we might assume that when artists actually painted outdoors, the pictorial development of naturalism would have been reinvigorated. On the contrary, it is perhaps shocking to be reminded that when painters went outdoors to paint what they actually saw, naturalism was abandoned. Painters had no need to make convincing illusions of what they could see and photograph.

———

This book recounts several crucial chapters in the history of seeing. Part 1 discusses the pictorial developments of the Western tradition beginning with the earliest recorded encounters between artist and landscape, namely, the efforts of the ancient Greeks. The discussion next moves through Roman and medieval times, and then concentrates on the most crucial convention in landscape depiction, the technique of linear perspective developed in the Renaissance. After that, it examines the "ideal" landscape painting of the seventeenth century, which is the culmination of these pictorial developments. Part 2, which describes the turning point in seeing the landscape pictorially, explains how these developments influenced the English landscape garden and picturesque vision more generally in the eighteenth century. Part 3, which deals with the naturalization, or assimilation into our culture, of pictorialization, describes the nineteenth and twentieth centuries, during which both the camera and the profession of landscape architecture came into existence. Two features of the nineteenth century are taken up: first, the popular landscape paintings designed to document America's "nature," and second, the late nineteenth-century abandonment of naturalistic painting. The final chapter discusses how naturalistic conventions have been translated into the actual landscape. This book closes with a look at various innovations in environmental design and painting that have taken place in our own century.

The landmarks discussed in this book have been chosen with an eye to answering one basic question: how did nature become pictorialized? They have been chosen by a landscape architect driven to study landscape painting by the need to question the basic terms of her profession. Knowledge of naturalistic paintings can teach us much about what conventions have given form to the landscape around us. Even further, it is possible that knowledge about these paintings can shatter the illusion that only what is familiar is natural.

Pictorial Developments | I

Confronting the Spectator: The Ancient World

2

This history of the pictorialization of the landscape, like so many histories, begins in Greece. The examples I discuss in this chapter, however, are not taken from landscape painting or pictures; they are from site planning.[1] I begin this way because there is no strong evidence that the earliest Greeks (prior to the fourth century B.C.E.) pictorialized their landscape at all. There are, in other words, simply no extant landscape pictures from that period. It is only in environmental design that we shall be able to understand the basic principles that animated the Greek conception of the landscape.

Precisely because these Greeks may not have miniaturized their landscape or reproduced it in pictorial form, studying their work provides us with a unique benefit: we shall be able to glimpse a conception of the landscape which, for us, is altogether unusual. As residents of the modern world we have been looking at landscape painting for two thousand years. It is an overwhelming distinction of the earliest Greeks, one that no later period can claim, that they may have experienced the landscape only in its actual size.

The unique—that is, nonpictorial—approach the Greeks took to their landscape has caused problems for modern viewers. A set of expectations based on modern ways of seeing has shaped the lens through which Greek sites have been observed and interpreted. As a result, scholars have argued that the Greeks did not care about, or design in response to, their landscape. One goal of this chapter, then, is to understand what happens when modern, or pictorial, expectations come into conflict with a nonpictorial approach to landscape.

Modern Expectations

One of the most striking tendencies seen in scholarship about Greek architecture is the widespread belief that during the archaic and classical periods (700–480 B.C.E. and 480–323 B.C.E., respectively), Greeks did not build their temples in any particular relationship to the land (3).[2] Modern scholars have written very little about, or even entirely dismissed, the relationship between the land and Greek constructions. Many who have studied Greek architecture for the past two hundred years have even concluded that the Greeks did not care about landscape (2). In *The Earth, the Temple, and the Gods,* Vincent Scully helps not only to refute this commonly held notion but also to clarify the basic presuppositions, or what I shall call the "scenic habits," that led scholars to make this mistake.

Briefly, Scully's point is this: scholars did not find a relationship between the land and temples because they were looking for something peculiarly modern: a pictorial relationship. This, it is true, did not exist. It does not follow, however, either that there was no relationship or that these ancient Greeks did not care about landscape. It only follows that they saw things differently.

The landscape of Greece is punctuated by moderate-sized and distinctly formed mountains that clearly define areas of valley and plain. These, in turn, serve as landmarks for orientation and provide enclosure for security. Unlike, for example, the midwestern United States, where the drifting observer must orient himself or herself primarily to the sky, or steeply mountainous regions, where the individual is engulfed in linear, directed valleys, Greece is a land where the mountains provide a sense of enclosure which is both outward and focused. It is in this landscape that the earliest Greeks sited their temples. And they did so, according to Scully, in relation to particular landscape features.

When modern scholars visited ancient sites they saw the remains of temples as beautiful sculptural ruins floating freely in the landscape (fig. 2.1). What they failed to see was a subtle relationship—created by the siting—that obtained between the temples and the landscape. This relationship took many shapes: a submissive nod to a greater force embodied in the land, a location already sacred, orientation to a particular landform, or a temple whose very form extended itself to the land. In all cases, the landscape and the buildings together formed a perceptually complete whole.

What modern observers of Greek temple sites had expected to see were their own culturally inherited conventions of how structures related to the land should look and should be sited. For example, a rather typical assumption was that forms and colors that differ strikingly from their surroundings are evidence that a design bears little or no relation to the landscape. The inverse of this notion is that forms and colors that blend with their surroundings are more respectful of nature or are somehow more natural. This, I suggest, is a modern, pictorially based, fallacy.

Consider, for example, this comment by Robert Scranton. After observing that in antiquity certain architectural forms were repeated in a variety of landscape contexts, he concludes that "in view of the rigid tradition of type forms of building, we find no variation in design that could be related to natural setting" (2).

Scully disagrees. The goal of his work is to demonstrate two re-

Fig. 2.1. Siting of a Greek Temple. Drawing by Mira Engler.

lated points. The first is that even though the building types were traditional, the temples varied depending on which god or goddess was being represented. "In point of fact, the historic Greeks partly inherited and partly developed an eye for certain surprisingly specific combinations of landscape features as expressive of particular holiness" (3). The second, is that Greek temples were always sited with an eye toward specific landscape features. Even though the buildings were distinct in color and form from the landscape, they were still formally related to it.

Modern viewers visiting ancient Greek temple ruins and considering their simple, abstract white forms, or imagining them as they were once painted with bright colors, might interpret this contrast with their surroundings to mean that they were designed to reject or negate their relationship to the land. It is unfair to assume, however, that design that attempts to look like, copy, or imitate what is truly natural (i.e., design that is naturalistic) is truly more respectful of nature. Designs that stand in sharp contrast to their surroundings uncompromisingly declare what they are: products of human or cultural intention. At the same time, such designs show an understanding that they are not natural. As a result, they might well disclose a deeper appreciation of both nature and design than do those designs that attempt to blend with their surroundings. Scully's view is something like this. The Greeks, he said, had a religion "in which the land was not a picture but a true force which physically embodied the powers that ruled the world" (3). Both the architecture and the site planning of the temples were meant not to imitate this force, but to acknowledge it.

Scully also objects to a second assumption that has characterized the study of Greek site planning: the position that forms that are "regularly" (e.g., symmetrically or geometrically) arranged in space are deliberately planned, while those that are disposed "irregularly" (e.g., with apparent disregard for geometrical order) are unplanned and haphazard. He argues that features considered unplanned at ancient temple sites actually corresponded to an organizational system that went unnoticed by modern eyes. To use a contemporary term, ancient temples were "site specific": they were designed to reveal the specific features of the particular landscape in which they were located. Furthermore, they were "god specific," created to embody the particular goddess or god being represented.

Scully provides for his thesis an extensive argument that is not really germane to this study.[3] The key point for us is, once again, that modern observers of Greek temple sites expected to see versions of their own culturally transmitted conventions. For example, they looked for axially directed views focused toward the frontal (picture) plane of a temple, with a diffuse landscape background. Our scenic habits have conditioned us to expect something like the neoclassical University of Virginia by Thomas Jefferson (fig. 2.2). Here the landscape is background to the "regularly" disposed, or staged, set of buildings facing the observer. Frontal views are provided, and these reflect back on and thus titillate the observer. The focus of the space created by the design showers the viewer with attention. Sight lines reverberate between the viewer and the dome rather than transmitting the viewer's attention beyond.

Not being similarly titillated at ancient sites and finding neither a frontal plane nor an axial approach directed toward them, modern scholars again concluded that Greek temples were not sited in relation to the land (3). Scully, however, argues that most Greek temples were, in fact, axially sited, with the axis extending not between the viewer and the structure but between the temple and a distinctly conical mountain feature. This landscape feature can be seen on the

Fig. 2.2. Siting of the University of Virginia. Drawing by Mira Engler.

route to the ancient temple at Knossos (fig. 2.3), the ancient town on the island of Crete.

This subtlety of site planning locates the modern viewer in an unfamiliar position, one that is outside of the composition, outside of the linear perspective inherited so assuredly since the Renaissance. Linear perspective is a method for reconstructing the spatial relations of objects as they might appear to an eye. It is based on an imaginary line drawn from one eye of the spectator to a vanishing point at the distant horizon. As we shall see in later chapters, linear perspective constitutes the essence of our scenic habits: views and prospects are determined by, and framed according to, the location of the spectator.

Scully argues that in early Greek sites the imaginary line was drawn not between the spectator and the temple but between the mountain and the temple. The ancient design, therefore, left the spectator out, and thus subordinated the viewer to the landscape. These archaic site-planning conventions may seem unnatural to us, for we are not in the habit of being left out of compositions. But the archaic ways are not unnatural: they are prepictorial. As such, they offer us an alternative mode of seeing, one that Scully describes as the "sculpturally real."

Unlike the approach to Jefferson's campus, the approach to an early Greek temple may have been more like experiencing a sculpture than a picture. The viewer walks up close to and all around a sculpture, using bodily movement to aid in the perception of form and depth. Shadows change as the viewer moves around, and the impression of form is heightened by each move. When experiencing a picture, only the viewer's *eyes* move about a frontal plane, trying to get as much information about the illusion of space and form as is possible from a single, detached point of view. Shadows are shown from only one direction and are exaggerated to give a convincing impression of three-dimensionality.

That modern scholars did not observe designed relationships between the temple and various landscape features illustrates the power pictorial seeing has had over us. We expect the world to appear to us as a picture does. Instead of meeting this expectation, the siting of archaic Greek temples depended on the space between the structure and the mountains. The observer had to move through the void to experience the tension between the two. The relationship of the early temples to the land followed regular patterns that illustrate how thoughtfully the landscape was observed.

It is illuminating to note that because of the absence of landscape illustration in ancient Greek drawings, some scholars have rejected the notion that the Greeks of the archaic and classical periods cared about landscape (2). A Greek vase (such as that shown in fig. 3.2) provides a straightforward example of ancient Greek painting: a line drawing that depicts figures and objects. There is no background and little, if any, depiction of space. Certainly there is no artificially composed view of the landscape, as there is in a typical landscape painting. Knowing, as we do, that the English word *landscape* originally meant an illusionistic view, we may speculate that the ancient Greeks did not care for artificially composed views of landscape. However, the fact that landscape was not depicted does not imply that the ancient Greeks did not have reverence for the land.

Still, some scholars argue that since the Greeks of the archaic and classical periods did not paint or carve representations of landscape they were also not interested in spatial relations. Take for example, the well-known text *Town and Square*. In it, Paul Zucker states that "the development of Greek vase painting, with the late and only very gradual introduction of perspective, may be considered a parallel proof of the lack of interest in space relations by the archaic Greek."[4] Zucker, I suggest, is like so many of us a victim of his scenic habits. He thinks that perspective is the only way to see the world, and thus assumes that because the Greeks didn't draw a line from a spectator's eye to a distant vanishing point, they didn't understand spatial relations. The fact is that perspective is a method for representing space in pictures. Zucker's accusation should therefore be reversed: how can we really understand spatial relations if we are so dependent on the perspective of two-dimensional pictures?

The very absence of miniaturized landscape backgrounds in vase paintings and reliefs may indicate that the Greeks of archaic and classical times cared deeply for the land. They had not experienced the sensation of seeing monumentally sized landscapes reduced to postcards. While we are thrilled, at least at first, by holding the image of a mountain range in the palm of our hand, the early Greeks may have only experienced mountains respectfully, at their full scale. They may not have considered the land something they had the power to reduce. Imagine, for a moment, what it might have been like to grow up without ever having seen a picture of a landscape, only the real thing.

Scully argues that it was only when belief in the goddesses and gods began to flag after the fourth century B.C.E. that picturesque poetry—nostalgic description of landscape delights—and landscape painting appeared. Even further, he argues that this same pattern was repeated in the eighteenth century: "Again it is only when the gods begin to die completely out of the lands and when many human beings begin to live lives totally divorced from nature—at the beginning, that is, of the modern age—that landscape painting, picturesque architecture, and landscape description, like that of the romantic discoverers of Greece itself, become the obsessive themes of art" (2).

As I have already briefly indicated, a good reason to study the ancient Greeks is that they might suggest to us an alternative way of seeing, the "sculpturally real." There is a second reason as well: within the development of Greek site planning itself we can observe a transition away from the sculpturally real and toward the pictorial. Not only does Greece provide an alternative, it also sows the seeds of the modern way of seeing.

Scully uncovers the following patterns in this development. Its first stage was the "sculpturally 'real,'" which was evidenced earliest in the Minoan civilization and culminated with the classical period. After this nonpictorial beginning, site-planning conventions in the late classical and then the Hellenistic periods became more internally organized: that is, structure related to structure, and structure confronted the viewer. This tendency he calls "the pictorially 'illusionistic'" (xii).

THE SCULPTURALLY REAL

The Minoan civilization flourished on the island of Crete from around 2000 B.C.E. to 1600 B.C.E. In the siting, orientation, and design of palaces, the Minoans made conscious use of the image and symbols of their most sacred goddess (11).[5] Theirs was a highly religious society, and a consistent and clearly defined pattern of land use can be recognized at every palace site. So far as possible, each palace was dependent on the same landforms: an enclosed valley within which the palace was set; a gently mounded hill on axis with the palace; and a higher, double-peaked mountain some distance beyond the hill but on the same axis. These forms defined a boundary that could have been seen at some distance from the palace.

The Minoan town complex and official palace at Knossos is a good example of the subordination of the palace to the landforms representing the goddess. Even from the old harbor, where the traveler of antiquity would have disembarked, the double peak of Mount Jouctas, a holy mountain that existed as a sacred site before the construction of the palace, can be seen rising directly to the south (fig. 2.3). One travels a serpentine path through the lower hills between the sea and Jouctas to arrive at the palace, which was clearly not fortified and merely rested in the security of a valley.

One does not approach Jouctas frontally. Only after following the labyrinthine path, accumulating spatial information, does one arrive in the central court of the palace, where the axis to the mountain of the goddess is revealed. This elaborate approach would seem to have fulfilled an important ceremonial function with great sensitivity to the sacred features of the landscape. Even a modern observer might dimly perceive what it must have been like to feel in harmony with, and at the mercy of, the spatial and temporal rhythms of the earth. Indeed, it is a rare occurrence today that we travel circuitously at a speed no faster than our own bodies can achieve. By contrast to the direct and the pictorial, this slow and labyrinthine path provides a valuable sculptural lesson.

A rising pattern of aggressiveness seems to characterize the culture generally referred to as Mycenean, which may have been responsible for the sack of Knossos about 1550 B.C.E. The Myceneans sited their fortresses in elevated positions on what had been considered the goddesses' hills. The view from the citadel of Mycenae itself (fig. 2.4) gives the best evidence that something had changed.

The citadel's fortified walls are in sharp contrast to the open Cretan palaces and clearly reveal its defensive posture. But the site-planning principle here suggests something more than just defense. The view from the summit of the citadel creates a sensation of physical and spiritual dominance over the landscape. In Mycenae we find a classic site-planning and pictorial lesson: elevated views looking out over the landscape empower the viewer.

—

Many centuries separate the Minoan and the Mycenaean constructions from the first Greek temples. (The archaic Greek period extended from about 700 B.C.E. to 480 B.C.E.) The majority of these temples are oriented toward the east, which means that existing landscape features had become subordinate to the rising sun. A movement away from the earth goddess to a sky god is thus clearly indicated.

The columned Greek temples are an unprecedented building form. The columns stand outside the temple walls and thereby extend the exterior space of the building out into the landscape. The transitional space they create directs the viewer's gaze to the horizon and receives the landscape from all directions. In this manner, the columns reinforce the spatial qualities of sculptural site planning that were discussed above.

At the same time, however, we can see an early sign of pictorialization: the columned temple composed views of the landscape. The columns may be described as framing members: they divide the actual landscape into a series of separate views seen by the spectator who is visiting the temple. Perhaps in some locations even the sacred mound and double peak were carefully framed for viewing. This very framing function in architecture will also be found in painting. We shall see, for example (fig. 3.4), that Roman landscape paintings were composed in a series of views looking out at the landscape, exactly as views would be seen between the columns of the temple.

To show how dramatically more pictorial the use of the columned

Fig. 2.3. Mount Jouctas from the ancient harbor of Knossos. Photograph by Vincent Scully.

Fig. 2.4. Mycenae. Photograph by Vincent Scully.

temple has become today, consider the typical neoclassical post office. Its sculptural spatial function has been lost. While the columns of the Greek temple framed the distant horizon in all directions, the post office is entirely frontal, with columns only across its street facade. In fact, rather than being designed to look out from, it is designed to be looked at by spectators—like a picture.

———

Zeus the King best represented the classical period. He asked his subjects to look above the distant mountains to the sky for authority. His most important temples were placed in the kinds of sites which had been most sacred to the goddess: the tops of the highest mountains and, to let the observer experience the bowl of the sky, the largest valleys (133).

According to Scully, probably the most harmonious of sites and therefore the one most reflective of Zeus is preserved in landform and stone at classical Olympia. It was designed sculpturally: the worshipper would not have seen the whole at once. Instead, it was necessary for the observer to follow a designed sequence, revealing aspects of the site in a cumulative, sculptural manner. The conical hill, which represented either the goddess or Kronos (the father of Zeus), would have been seen first. The brightly stuccoed bulk of the temple of Zeus would then have risen higher up as a balancing element. The temple of Zeus, well out in space and away from the hill, opposed the old way and stood above the route to the stadium where the sacred contests were carried on in his name.

The next thing the spectator would have seen at Olympia was the temple of Hera in relation to the conical hill and the temple of Zeus. Unlike the temple of Zeus, whose form was high, broad, compact, and dense, the temple of Hera hugs the ground and is purposefully long, low, and open. At the center of the site, the observer stands in a calm and ample outdoor room defined by the temple of Hera to the north and the temple of Zeus to the south. This "room" is what designers typically call "space-positive" design, in which structures relate to other structures in order to form clearly defined outdoor rooms. Yet this example differs from today's outdoor rooms in one important respect: the structures facing the ancient room are not parallel.

The spatial form defined by the temples of Hera and Zeus is strong, and one thinks the temples are parallel, as they almost are. But the eye perceives that they are not; they are active forces pressing in upon the space between them. The eye, under the prodding of the mind, is constantly attempting to make them parallel in order to release the pressure of the difference. From this movement they appear to be actively engaged with one another (151). This active engagement is the result of the coordination between what the eye sees and what the body experiences in space. Spatial tension must be experienced at the actual site. Pictures will not—and, indeed, cannot—substitute.

The really extraordinary point about this site design is that no camera can photograph these two temples at once from the center of the "room." This tells us about the encompassing spatial and sculptural emphasis that characterizes this site. In practical contemporary terms, if a photograph of such a "room" were entered in a professional competition, it would not fare well. By contrast, a frontal and more pictorial siting, such as that of the modern post office, would do nicely. The rather simple question, Does a site photograph easily? thus becomes a test of whether a design is pictorial or sculptural. (This is why, by the way, I don't include photographs of these temples.)⁶

THE PICTORIALLY ILLUSIONISTIC

In late classical times, there occurred three extraordinary developments in the history of seeing pictorially: the gridded street system, the use of the building as a frontally sited space definer, and the space-positive form of the agora (or marketplace). They are exceptional breaks from the past because each of these pictorial devices turns abruptly to confront the spectator, who, no longer needing to move to experience a temple or space, is now practically stationary. All of these conventions, still in use today, are giant steps toward pictorial design.

The earliest examples of the gridded street system, thought to have been invented by Hippodamos, were produced between 470 B.C.E. and 430 B.C.E.⁷ The grid, whether in a city or on the background of a contemporary poster, unifies forms that otherwise are independent. Distant mountains may have been "natural" boundaries for cities, but the grid created additional boundaries—economic and political ones. This purely geometric control of space could be used to plan cities with only minimal regard for landforms. Such rationalized site planning occurred in cities where sacred conventions were not as strong as at temple sites such as those already mentioned.

Scully concludes that owing to the grid, cities were forced to use devices of an almost "picturesque" character to retain the visual relationships with the land which had been so highly valued. A pedestrian following an important axis of a grid, for example, would see the city's theater in one direction and, turning the opposite way, would see a sacred landform in the other. What does Scully mean by "picturesque" when he refers to site planning based on the grid? "[Site planning as a device] was often concerned with dramatic or idyllic views at least partly for their own sake, and with effects of visual relief, surprise, and atmosphere which were sometimes theatri-

cal, sentimental or forced" (188). These are exactly the effects we
shall discover again and again in pictorial development. In particular,
as we shall see later on, surprise and visual relief are most notably
associated with the picturesque movement and the landscape garden
of the eighteenth century.

It should not be too surprising that the next dramatic development
was the frontally designed building—it now faced the gridded street.
Scully associates Hippodamos with the first frontal siting, that of the
Hephaisteon, the temple of Hephaistos and Athena (fig. 2.5), built in
Athens around 444 B.C.E. (189). That this temple is oriented and designed to be seen from the front is evidenced by the presence of a
detailed pediment on the front which is lacking on the other three
sides. The temple's excellent state of preservation makes it easy to
see, even today, that any view, except from the east front, is surprisingly unsatisfactory. The temple entirely fails as a sculptural body
and, instead, is frontally designed and pictorially sited. As is obvious,
it photographs well.

Fig. 2.5. Hephaisteion, approximately as seen in ancient frontal approach. Photograph
by Vincent Scully.

There is always a problem that accompanies frontally designed buildings: the three other sides can distract the viewer from the front facade. Consequently, devices are needed to deemphasize the remaining sides. What is really fascinating about this particular example is that the ancient solution to the problem of deemphasizing the body of the structure is identical to a common modern one: foundation planting. By its very nature, the foundation planting is nonspatial. That is, the plants simply reinforce the plane against which they rest. The need to mask, or further deemphasize, three sides of the temple of Hephaistos and Athena must have been recognized during the third century B.C.E., when shrubs were planted at regular intervals around the south, west, and north sides of the building (189). They helped to disguise the body of the building and compress it into a two-dimensional facade. Foundation plantings help to reinforce a singular view from the agora (or today's suburban street), where the spectator can be fixed in place for viewing such facades.

The temple of Hephaistos and Athena was meant to be seen from the agora, and it is extraordinarily effective in that view (190). The absence of the foundation planting at the front further reinforces the spatial function of the agora. It restricts access from the three sides that are planted and encourages access in front. The agora thereby becomes the body of the temple. This is confirmed by the sequential experiences of the pedestrian. Entering straight into the room of the front porch, the spectator, after paying his or her respects to the deities, would have turned to look back across the center of the city and would have seen a view of the city which was carefully designed and framed, like a modern picture-postcard view.

The third development in pictorial site planning, the agora, was informed by the previous two: the agora was a space bounded by the grid and by frontally designed buildings. Looking at a reconstruction of a site in Assos (fig. 2.6), we can see that the stoa defines the space of the agora. The stoa, a type of building fronted by a long porch, was an invention of the archaic period but became an essential instrument of Hellenistic design. It is planned according to principles in which the space dominates; the building's overall form gives precedence to the space it forms. The stoa regularizes exterior space and is itself an urban landscape boundary. As the stoa becomes a definer of space its architectural details recede, since the emphasis is on the unity of the space rather than on the solid form (191).

The agora represents a significant development in the history of pictorialization for two important reasons: it places the spectator perpendicular to the frontally designed building, and it creates a space that can be wholly viewed without moving. These conditions are quite the opposite of the "sculpturally real" design, which relied on the spectator to accumulate spatial information.[8]

For good reason, urban designers look to the agora as the first

Fig. 2.6. Agora at Assos (reconstruction). From F. H. Bacon, ed., *Investigations at Assos* (Cambridge, Massachusetts, 1902).

great model of space-positive design for cities. It has been copied by some of the greatest public spaces: piazzas, squares, and malls. Each uses buildings to sculpt exterior space, creating what might be termed "stage space" for pedestrians. Like a picture, a stage assumes that the viewer is fixed in a single location and does not need to move or to accumulate spatial information. Indeed, both the stage and the theater were to be crucial in the development of pictorial illusion.

———

The ancient chapter of the history of landscape design is extraordinarily rich. In its earliest periods, before the fourth century B.C.E., it provides a premodern mode of seeing, described by Scully as the "sculpturally real," in which mystery, cumulative experience, and revelation rule, and which is a genuine alternative to the mode with which we have become familiar. By the late classical period, the Greeks began to discover the basic principles of pictorialization: unity, balance, and the pleasure and power derived from seeing an entire panorama from a distance. The products of a pictorial attitude included elevated views, the formation of space to control the spectator's movement, the use of the foundation planting to strengthen the frontal design of buildings, and the unification of a composition that immobilizes the spectator and thereby favors, freezes, and frames particular views, or pictures, of the landscape. Before being presented with actual pictures, however, the spectator had to face another unified composition: the stage.

Staging the Spectacle: Hellenistic and Roman Times

3

The Greek stage employed compositional conventions that were inherited by Roman painters and used by them to depict the landscape. Thus, for the first time, the landscape was "designed," reproduced, and miniaturized. A process was set into motion, one from which there was no turning back: never again would the landscape be experienced only at full scale as the earliest Greeks had experienced it.

Landscape painters not only inherited compositional conventions from the stage but maintained them throughout the Middle Ages and kept them ready for Renaissance perspective. As we know from the outward views that were designed into Renaissance gardens, this series of transitions—from site to stage to painting—eventually moved back to sites.

Now we shall turn to the Greek theater. As we do so, remember how often the word *scenery* is used to denote the landscape. Most of us have probably heard someone say, "We saw beautiful scenery on our trip to the coast." Let us not forget that *scenery* is a word taken from theater, and that the view seen from the car window is thus unselfconsciously assumed to be like a stage setting. This is hardly accidental, for indeed the stage played a crucial role in the development of our scenic habits.

Greek Theaters

Because of its prominent location in the overall design of ancient cities, the theater itself provides an important example of the "pictorially illusionistic." Often, the theater functioned as one terminus of the city's major axis, while, in some cities at least, the other was a distant and sacred landform. The city itself was carefully designed so that its inhabitants could orient themselves between two scenic views: the stage, and dramatic landforms.

The site of Megalopolis reveals the role theaters played in the layout of cities. Literally meaning "great city," the name *megalopolis*, the origin of our word for conglomerations of cities, designated a massive urban center uniting forty villages. This settlement was therefore a supremely artificial creation set down in the center of a plain without the benefit of traditional siting or ancient sanctity. Laid out in a Hippodamian grid in 371 B.C.E., it seems to have used both the grid and its theater as primary devices for bringing the city and distant landforms together. The theater is oriented directly toward the single high conical peak. Near the peak is a cleft in the ridge which might be interpreted as a rather indefinite pair of horns.[1]

An axis was thus created between the sacred landforms and the city's theater, and along this axis were located all the holiest places of the city. In traveling from one holy place to another, the spectator would walk either toward the theater or toward the sacred mountain.[2] On the basis of this description of Megalopolis, we can identify the postclassical use of the grid and the axis. Both of them are frontal and perpendicular, and they act as pictorial devices in the planning of an entire city by placing the spectator within their geometrical arrangement. At the same time, they also preserve the archaic tradition of orienting buildings to sacred landforms.

Much more important than the fact that theaters played a role in the layout of cities is the manner in which theater design developed, and the influence it had on later centuries. For example, one scholar describes the visual arts of the Renaissance as follows: "Those patterns and conventions were merely varying adaptations of the art traditions of centuries, most of them dating, in fact, from the Hellenistic period when painters and sculptors were imitating the Greek theater."[3] Most of us readily acknowledge the importance of the Renaissance to the development of the visual arts of the West. Now we must look to the Greek theater as an important source of that era's earliest and most enduring patterns and conventions.

The Greek word for theater is *theatron*; it is related to various words for seeing, including *thea* (sight or spectacle). The spectacle provided by early theaters was, in fact, the sight of the dramatically formed valley-and-plain landscape native to Greece, as exemplified at Epidauros (fig. 3.1). Built into hillsides, theaters were always half open so that spectators were surrounded by a wide arc of distant landforms. Indeed, this is the first example of the landscape acting literally as "scenery." That we often call the landscape "scenic" implies that we both interpret and construct our landscape in accordance with models derived from the theater. Many pictorial conventions for unifying a scene, as we shall see, are adaptations dating from the Hellenistic period, when painters and sculptors imitated the Greek theater.

Today the word *scenery* is even used interchangeably with *landscape*. To use the word *scene* to denote stage sets or views represented in pictures is analogous to using the word *figure* to denote a person in a picture. But to use the word *scene* to describe views in the real world should seem as strange as calling a real person in a park a *figure*. Yet we commonly hear the landscape referred to as scenery, as though it were a picture or a stage. What we are actually doing when we refer to the landscape as scenery is reflecting our scenic habits by recognizing, even unconsciously, the compositional conventions that make some views "scenic."

Although the notion of landscape as scenery may not seem shocking to us today, this is only because we have become accustomed to this particular conception of the landscape. The very word *scenic* presupposes a boundary around a particular view. It is as if, in particular places, the landscape were a painting or a stage set, separated from its less-than-scenic surroundings. But how do we distinguish what is scenic from what is less so? The process of defining a boundary to designate a view is not natural, god-given, automatic, or absolute; it is learned. The boundaries that define works of art have al-

Fig. 3.1. Theater at Epidauros, view looking northward. Photograph by Vincent Scully.

ready been determined by the artists or designers, and it is these that function as our primary sources when we learn where to locate boundaries when looking out at the actual world or redesigning its landscape.

Why do we assume that the landscape is, or ought to be, scenic? The assumption is so deeply engrained that the question may sound strange. Describing the landscape as scenic implies, by analogy, that it is a backdrop or background. Accordingly, one must ask, a background to what? Certainly the answer is that the landscape is a background to the dramatic actions of people, of society, even of culture itself. This conception of the landscape separates people from the environment they inhabit and modify. More important to the present study is that this structural relation between a scenic landscape and the people who view it is the same as the relation between a spectator and a painting. Both imply a certain distance between subject and object, a separation that allows people to view landscape as a patron would view a work of art.

One of the most important characteristics of a scene in theater is its use of boundaries to create a unified composition. Not only did the actual landscape serve as a background to theaters in ancient times but the theater itself helped to establish the conditions for a unified composition by locating an immobile spectator in relation to itself. The seated spectator could relax comfortably and behold a dramatic scene. The result of this orientation was that the stage and landscape together became a frontally designed scene—once again, like a picture. For our purposes, this is the most significant fact about the Hellenistic discovery of the unified composition, for this scenic convention is readily transferred to landscape painting.

Hellenistic Stage Design

During the Hellenistic period, roughly 323 B.C.E. to 30 B.C.E., theater designers organized their stages with a particular device called the "stage screen."[4] This screen is important for us to look at because it essentially became the picture plane on which an illusionary space was constructed in painting. Its organizing principles became the lens through which even today we choose actual scenic views in the landscape.

The stage screen of Hellenistic theaters served as a humanly scaled backdrop for the actors. Basically just a wall with openings, the first screens probably did little more than unite doorways for the actors into a single design that symbolized a building (e.g., a temple). The stage screen was embellished with columns and pediments that framed the entrance doors and divided the screen into panels. In later centuries, when painters, sculptors, and architects used niches, columns, and pediments to unite carved figures, they were borrowing from the ancient stage screen. (See, e.g., fig. 5.3, which shows an early Renaissance painting by Lippi.)

The stage screen was much more than simply a decorative wall. Since, as we have already seen, the ancient Greek theaters were situated outdoors, stage designers needed a device that would signify interior space. The stage screen served precisely this function. According to the first-century Roman writer Vitruvius, Greek theaters had been planned with three centers of action.[5] These may well correspond to three parts of the stage screen: the central section, and two projecting wings at the side, called *parascenia*. First the central section and later the projecting wings took on the role of signifying interior space.

The central section housed interior space by becoming a "pavilion"—our word for a shelter in a park or garden. Figure 3.2 shows

Fig. 3.2. Medea vase (detail). Bruckmann München Bildarchiv, Munich.

scenes from the play *Medea,* as illustrated on an ancient Greek vase. We can see how the central pavilion acts as an interior shelter for the location of particular events in the play. It is shown floating within the linearly illustrated events, which seem to follow the path of a processional play or the narrative of a book.

The central pavilion (often with a curtain to reinforce it), successfully served the function of defining interior space and centering compositions until well into the Renaissance, but it failed to define exterior space. A great leap in pictorial development occurred when the projecting wings rather than the central section were used to define interior space: an opening was created for illusory landscapes.

Placing something (e.g., a pavilion) in the middle of a space leaves the surrounding space undefined, left over. To unify and thereby take control of exterior space, boundaries are required. The projecting wings of the stage screen fulfilled this important function. Like enormous arms enclosing space, or gates defining openings, the wings of the stage framed an exterior room at the same time as they themselves could be used for interior scenes. They strengthened enclosure and gave the illusion of greater depth than could otherwise be achieved in the narrow scope of the stage.

"Coulisse" is the convention for enclosing space within the wings of the stage and, more generally, for creating a corridor. As we shall see, the convention of coulisse was transferred from the stage to painting. (See figs. 4.4 and 5.1 for examples of the early uses of projecting wings as side houses in a Byzantine mosaic and a fourteenth-century fresco, respectively.) Through a complex development (which will be discussed in later chapters), coulisse was then actually used in the design of eighteenth-century gardens, in which spaces were defined by clumps of trees (fig. 3.3). This convention is still used in gardens and parks, in which clumps of trees echo one another and define vistas; its purpose is to create scenic effects, particularly to frame space and give the illusion of greater distance. Thus the conventions used in designing our parks, far from being natural, are descendants of the conventions of stage design.

Each of these changes in the stage screen contributed to pictorial

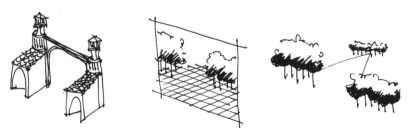

Fig. 3.3. Coulisse on stage, in painting, in landscape.

organization by unifying compositions and strengthening the illusion
of space. Indeed, the stage screen had become the plane to which space
was related, and as noted above, it would become the picture plane
through which painted illusions would be unified. Painting inherited
from early theaters not only the "screen," with its central pavilion
and side houses for enclosing space and giving the illusion of more
depth, but also the very idea that the illusion was set outdoors. Ancient stage producers needed to create interior scenes to complement
landscape scenes that, of course, were already provided by the exterior setting of the theater itself. A student of late medieval or early
Renaissance painting is struck immediately by the fact that no matter
what type of subject is represented, the painter has assumed an exterior point of view, since the buildings are always shown as exteriors.
It may seem obvious that the landscape is the staged setting for cultural expression, but what all these conventions together succeed in
doing is strengthening a particular way of looking at the landscape: a
view as seen by a stationary spectator.

Roman Prospects

A literally pictorial development in the history of the stage screen
was the fact that it became painted—an illusionary surface itself. After the fourth century B.C.E., the Greek stage screen became so high
as to block the view of the landscape. At about that time, panels
painted with illusionary perspectives were set into grooves between
the columns. Many of these paintings depicted, for the first time ever,
landscapes. Painted landscapes replaced sacred landforms. There are
no existing Greek panels for us to see, but according to Vitruvius the
Romans painted in their homes scenes that imitated those painted for
the stage by the ancient Greeks.[6] We shall now take a look at one of
those Roman paintings to get a sense of how actual landscapes were
replaced by representations.

    The Arrival of Ulysses in the Land of the Laestrygonians (fig. 3.4)
is one of seven existing panels from the Odyssey Landscapes, which
illustrates the mythical adventure of Odysseus about which Homer
wrote in the eighth century B.C.E. A Roman family in the middle of
the first century B.C.E. may have commissioned it for their home. The
separate scenes would have provided a thrilling landscape spectacle
painted on the upper walls of a room, or, since they may have been
imitations of earlier stage panels, on the Hellenistic stage itself.

    Columns and pilasters adopted from both the temple and the stage
screen were painted on the wall to enframe the continuous prospect.
The red-and-gold pilasters are trompe l'oeils: painted to give the illusion of being three-dimensional. We know that just such real red
columns or half-columns were used to hold and separate the painted

Fig. 3.4. *The Arrival of Ulysses in the Land of the Laestrygonians,* a Hellenistic fresco from the Odyssey Landscapes (late first century B.C.E.). Museo Profano, Vatican. (Alinari/Art Resource, New York.)

stage panels.[7] These framing conventions do more than provide a boundary for the paintings: these deceptive pilasters further increase the illusion of a real view in the same way a window frames a view outside. They are in effect the earliest convention for creating the "window aesthetic" so intimately associated with Western culture.

Illusionistic art of this sort provides a window to the world which accomplishes a pleasing deception: it gives us the impression that we are looking at the actual landscape when, of course, we are not. By comparing this painting with the text that inspired it, we shall see (following closely the interpretation of Eleanor Winsor Leach) that the painter has used a good measure of artistic license to fill out the landscape and incorporate some visual tricks.

First, however, before going to the text, let us simply observe the spatial qualities of the painting. The Odyssey Landscapes exemplifies a panoramic view of landscape. (The word *panorama* is derived from *pan,* a Greek word meaning all or every, and *horan,* meaning to see.) Together the panels provide the illusion of open and unconstrained landscape—the most extensive view we know of for the time.

The technique of perspective used in the Odyssey Landscapes produces an illusion of spatial recession through the diminution of background figures and the impressionistic technique of making colors less intense as they approach the horizon. Through the use of coulisse, depth is further increased: deep vistas are framed by trees and rock outcrops. Roman methods of simulating spatial recession do not produce a perfectly systematized illusion (like that found in Renaissance painting) to control the spectator's point of view. Rather, they offer an informative approximation of an illusion, toward which spectators must establish their own point of view (41–42).[8]

In the *Odyssey* the reader is scarcely given enough information to assemble a comprehensive picture of a landscape. In the description of Odysseus's arrival in the land of the Laestrygonians, individual landscape features are incorporated into the narrative only to prepare the reader for the outcome of the adventure:

> There as we entered the glorious harbor, which a sky-towering
> cliff encloses on either side, with no break anywhere,
> and two projecting promontories facing each other
> run out toward the mouth, and there is a narrow entrance,
> there all the rest of them had their oar-swept ships in the inward
> part, they were tied up close together inside the hollow
> harbor, for there was never a swell of surf inside it,
> neither great nor small, but there was a pale calm on it.
> I myself, however, kept my black ship on the outside,
> at the very end, making her fast to the cliff with a cable,
> and climbed to a rocky point of observation and stood there.
> From here no trace of cattle nor working of men was visible;
> all we could see was the smoke going up from the country.
> So I sent companions ahead telling them to find out
> what men, eaters of bread, might live here in this country.
> I chose two men, and sent a third with them, as a herald.
> (*Odyssey* 10.87–102)[9]

By mentioning towering cliffs, unbroken crags, and a narrow entrance to the harbor, Homer prepares the reader to see how the ships of Odysseus's companions come to be trapped by the Laestrygonians while Odysseus himself is able to escape because of his foresight in anchoring outside.

The painter of the Odyssey Landscapes, however, produced an image of the Laestrygonian harbor by superimposing a spatial structure on the inexplicit territory of Homer's tale. His use of spatial recession and full articulation of topography is one of the greatest pictorial innovations of the early Roman period. Yet the spectator might wonder if the painter had read the same text of the *Odyssey* that we know today.

In *The Arrival of Ulysses in the Land of the Laestrygonians* two massive rock outcrops mark the entrance to the harbor, and trees delineate the distant shoreline. Several ships dock in the inner harbor, Odysseus's three companions stand in front of a cave meeting a Laestrygonian princess, another female figure personifies a spring, two sheep stand near the shore, and cattle can be seen in the distance. In the *Odyssey*, however, no one can be seen from the harbor. Instead, the sailors meet the princess at an inland spring outside the city gates. Why would the painter depict the events so differently? Certainly by compressing many events into one scene he can illustrate more of the adventure. However, Leach makes an additional argument, which tells us about the pictorial innovation that paintings such as the Odyssey Landscapes typify: the preservation of foreground continuity across succeeding panels to support the illusion of a landscape as if seen through window frames (38).

To create such an illusion, the painter has interpolated a panorama to fill the distance between the shore in the foreground of this panel and the city in the horizon of the next. In other words, the painter has adjusted Homer's tale to create a panorama from isolated events. The topography the painter has created, however, is not entirely imagined. "In explaining the particular topographical phenomena of the frieze—its steep cliffs, stark dolmens, and jagged harbors—scholars have often referred to the long-standing tradition that identifies the territory of Odysseus's wanderings with Sicily and the western coast of Southern Italy" (55).

Yet this view is certainly not a specific view of Italy that the painter was observing while painting. Its actual design is constructed to inform the spectator about the text. The isolated cliff presents an "image of a wild and lonely place calculated to intimate danger. The iconography of the scene makes the intimations explicit. The forms of Odysseus's three companions stand out sharply against the dark mouth of a cave beneath an overhanging brow of a cliff. There is no Homeric basis for this cave, but there is a strong basis in visual tradition. Rocky arches that symbolize the entrance to the underworld appear frequently in South Italian vase painting to surround figures doomed to death—as these three comrades of Odysseus are" (39). The two rocky outcrops look like dolmens, prehistoric monuments thought to mark grave sites. The cliff, the cave, and the dolmens therefore are designed not only as a geographical reference but also as a symbolic and compositional center for the painting.

The space between the shore and city has been designated by the painter as a pastoral landscape. We see placid sheep near the shore and cattle herding in the sunlit plain even though in the *Odyssey* Odysseus specifically said that he saw no animals. The creation of pastoral landscapes where none existed before has been a staple of landscape architecture. But why would the painter have pictured a pasture even in contradiction to Homer's text? Of course we don't know the answer, but we do know that Virgil's pastoral poetry was emerging at about the time that the Odyssey Landscapes were being painted, and therefore it is at least conceivable that Virgil's pastoral poetry and the painting of his day were reinforcing one another.

Leach makes a very convincing argument that the pictorial richness of Virgil's poetry may have been based on a thorough understanding of a Roman innovation in the history of seeing: the reader's ability to conceptualize a unified visual space (40). To make such a claim, Leach compares Homer's description of Odysseus's arrival in the Laestrygonian harbor with Virgil's description of a topographically similar harbor. In Homer's description, "the landscape achieves a distinct form that the modern reader may well pause to imagine. Whether Homer's contemporary listener thus conceived a mental image we can hardly surmise, but such an activity is not dictated by the narrative. At no point in his building of the image does Homer himself reflect upon its totality or fill the space between the headland and the cave . . . [Instead] Homer's harbor description is a mythic paradigm that associates the physical features of the hero's homeland with the internal structure of his personality" (32, 34).

In Virgil's description, however, the features of the landscape are united within a broad panorama. Virgil fills in the topography as if painting a picture. Homer's description moves the eye forward, while Virgil's directs the reader's attention up and down in space to contemplate the interrelation of objects. Further, in Virgil's text "the details are not seen from the point of view of one moving past them in space, but rather from a fixed location at the harbor mouth" (33). From this description we see a change not unlike the change from the sculpturally real to the pictorially illusionistic which we observed among the ancient Greeks. The viewer is no longer moving along a path and accumulating details but is fixing upon a particular and distant point of view from which to observe the whole picture. If this is true, then Virgil recognized what his contemporary readers had learned from pictures: the ability to conceptualize space.

The Pastoral Ideal

Not only was Virgil one of the first poets to write about the landscape in scenic and pictorial terms but the legacy of his pastoral ideal has been a significant influence upon environmental design for centuries. Although pastoral poems were written centuries before him, Virgil succeeded in describing landscapes in memorable terms that are still with us. What inspired Virgil's scenic landscape description? Some scholars conclude that it might have been painting.[10] At the time Virgil was writing, Homer's very brief landscape references in the *Odyssey* were being heroically pictured on the walls of the homes of the Roman aristocracy. It is therefore possible that the Odyssey Landscapes themselves were the inspiration for Virgil's pictorially illusionistic landscape descriptions. If so, then we would surely have a wonderful example of how pictures influence not just the way we see the landscape but also the way we talk about it. (The way we talk, of course, influences the way we see.)

Virgil translated the pastoral from Greek to Latin in his *Eclogues,* and he transported its landscape from Sicily to an imaginary place he called Arcadia.[11] Though he is rarely found in the core curricula for a general education today, Virgil is frequently mentioned in histories of landscape architecture, in which phrases such as "Arcadian scenes," "idyllic landscapes of the pastoral tradition," and "Virgilian landscapes" are common. Pastoral design is one of the most enduring and popular forms of landscape architecture. Consider, for example, its importance to Olmsted, the founder of landscape architecture in the United States. In conceiving of Central Park, he stated, "It should be given such a character as, while affording contrast and variety of scene, would as much as possible be confluent to the same end, namely, the constant suggestion to the imagination of an unlimited range of rural conditions . . . Considering that large classes of rural objects and many types of natural scenery are not practicable to be introduced on the site of the Park,—mountain, ocean, desert, and prairie scenery for example,—it will be found that the most valuable form that could have been prescribed is that which may be distinguished from all others as pastoral."[12]

The pastoral is essentially rural and reflective of the life of shepherds. The association of landscape architecture with the rural is so intimate that one prominent historian even limits the definition of *landscape* to that which is rural.[13] Virgil's pastoral, however, was an ideal landscape that represented a comfortable respite from real life and has been a powerful influence on both European and American attitudes toward landscape. We shall see that in the sixteenth and seventeenth centuries this symbolic landscape was first transmitted to Europeans through painting. Giorgione and Claude Lorrain, for example, were explicit in their depiction of Virgilian scenes. Later, these painterly images took actual form in grass and trees in the English landscape garden. Even with such an extremely brief chronological sketch, the enormous power of the Virgilian poem in shaping the landscape should be clear.

Because of its great influence, we shall next examine a good portion of Virgil's first eclogue.[14] The poem takes the form of a dialogue between two shepherds, Tityrus and Meliboeus, whose fortunes are quite different. Tityrus enjoys rural leisure, while Meliboeus, who speaks first, has been exiled from his farm:

> Tityrus, while you lie there at ease under the awning of a spreading beech and practice country songs on a light shepherd's pipe, I have to bid good-bye to the home fields and the ploughlands that I love. Exile for me, Tityrus—and you lie sprawling in the

shade, teaching the woods to echo back the charms of Amaryllis. (lines 1–5)

Tityrus embodies the pastoral ideal, lying at ease in a meadow under a beech tree, playing his pipe. He seems to have no work to do. His relationship with his environment can best be understood by the fact that when he plays music, the woods echo back the sounds from his pipe. His environment not only satisfies his every need but obeys his commands.

Tityrus explains how a Roman has given him leisure and sanctioned the continuity of his peaceful world:

Ah Meliboeus, the man to whom I owe this happy leisure is a god. Yes, I shall always treat him as a god. He shall have an altar, and I will often stain it with the blood of a young lamb from my fold. See for yourself. He gave the word—and my cattle browse at large, while I myself can play the tunes I fancy on my rustic flute. (lines 6–10)

Tityrus's restful world is represented by the luxuriant shelter of the beech tree, and the pasture where animals are free to graze. This is the ideal landscape of the Virgilian pastoral, which has been represented in the landscape garden and our own parks. It is easy to see why this ideal place has been the source of dreams for two thousand years. Indeed, we could picture Tityrus comfortably resting in the pastoral forms of our own Central Park. By reading further, however, we will see that this representation is as misleading as are today's imitations of Tityrus's pasture; the remainder of the poem will modify, if not entirely obliterate, the bland felicity of the opening image.

Tityrus's farm is a place salvaged from the continuing struggle between nature (*natura*) and civilization (*humana*). It introduces the reader to a world where people no longer live in instinctive harmony with their surroundings but must secure and defend the order they have made. What surrounds Tityrus's pastoral ideal? Representatives of nature and civilization: on one side the city of Rome, and on the other a swamp that might invade the pasture at any time.

Happy old man! So your land will still be yours. And it's enough for you, even though the bare rock and the marshland with its mud and reeds encroach on all your pastures. (lines 46–49)

"Throughout the poem, the farm landscape is the only prospect seen directly and in detail, the center of the world the poet is creating, yet always we look obliquely beyond it to the suggestions of chaos on its borders. Thus the farm incorporates two modes of existence: it is at once a self-contained, harmonious microcosm, the symbol of a well-balanced life, and a location within the greater world of harsh, demanding nature."[15]

To protect it from outside threats the farm is enclosed by streams and hedges that serve as barriers against the chaos outside. Within these boundaries that signify personal ownership, the farm may appear ideal. "Intermingled activities blend separate activities into an harmonious whole. The leaf-cutter sings at his work, the bees lull the herdsman to sleep; the birds respond to his care. Such harmony is the result of human organization."[16]

> Happy old man! You will stay here, between the rivers that you know so well, by springs that have their Nymphs, and find some cool spot underneath the trees. Time and again, as it has always done, the hedge there, leading from your neighbour's land, will have its willow-blossom rifled by Hyblaean bees and coax you with a gentle humming through the gates of sleep. On the other side, at the foot of the high rock, you will have the vine-dresser singing to the breezes; while all the time your dear full-throated pigeons will be heard, and the turtle-dove high in the elm will never bring her cooing to an end. (lines 51–58)

At the end of the poem, the other boundary is identified when Tityrus looks toward the hills that form his horizon, casting long shadows over the valley. Like the streams and hedges, the hills also serve as a protective barrier, enclosing a small cluster of farms and houses, but they also mark the beginning of the great world—beyond them lies Rome.

> See over there—the rooftops of the farms are already putting up their evening smoke and shadows of the mountain crests are falling farther out. (lines 82–84)

The shadows from the larger world are cast over the pasture that looked so inviting in the sun. The evening fires are protection against the immediate environment as well as the distant and unknown.

Tityrus has been to Rome, however, to buy his freedom from slavery. Before going, he had in his ignorance believed in a homogeneous world. Now experience forces him to reckon with differences and contrasts:

> I was a simpleton, Meliboeus. I used to think that the city they call Rome was like our markettown, where we shepherds are accustomed to drive down our new-weaned lambs. Arguing from what I knew, from a dog's likeness to a puppy and a goat's to her kids, I measured big by little things. But I soon saw that Rome stands out above all other cities as the cypress soars above the drooping undergrowth. (lines 19–25)

The sight of Rome has dazzled the old shepherd, but he still chooses to return to the country. Tityrus believes that he has gained a vision of world order. In the security of his pastoral setting and with his freedom, he can readily believe that the order of his own life typifies the order of the universe. Consequently, he settles back into the easy complacency of a sentimental pastoralist, becoming, in some respects, the dreamer that he had first seemed to Meliboeus. Thus now it is Meliboeus who has most to reveal of the relationship between the pastoral world and the chaos outside.

Meliboeus is understandably angry and perplexed about his exile from the ideal pasture:

> Don't think I am jealous. *My* only feeling is amazement—with every farm in the whole countryside in such a state of chaos. Look at myself, unfit for the road, yet forced to drive my goats on this unending trek. See, Tityrus, I can hardly drag this one along. Just now, in the hazel thicket here, she bore two kids—I had been counting on them—and had to leave the poor things on the naked flints. Ah, if I had not been so blind, I might have known that we were in for this disaster. Often enough I had been warned by Heaven, when lightning struck the oaks. (lines 11–17)

Meliboeus has told us that everywhere beyond the pasture is chaos. Even life itself is threatened—the sheep has left her offspring, and thunderbolts have spoken of danger.

While Tityrus, secure in the pastoral setting, was talking about Rome, Meliboeus, who has been evicted from his land by the Roman government, reminisces about the farm he has left. Will sacrilegious soldiers and barbarians take over his pasture?

> Is some blaspheming soldier to own these acres I have broken up and tilled so well—a foreigner, to reap these splendid fields of corn? Look at the misery to which we have sunk since Romans took to fighting one another. To think that *we* have sown, for men like that to reap! Yes, Meliboeus, now graft your pears; now plant a row of vines!
>
> Forward, my goats; forward, the flock that used to be my pride. Never again, stretched out in some green hollow, shall I spy you far away, dangling on the rocky hillside where the brambles grow. There will be no songs from me, my goats, and I shall lead you no more to crop the flowering clover and the bitter willow shoots. (lines 70–78)

For Meliboeus, the world is an image of chaos. Before his exile, he had believed in the orderly maintenance of the farm; now he has the feeling that there is no order anywhere in the world. As farmer and shepherd, he had seeded his lands, grafted his trees, clipped his vines, yet apparently produced no indissoluble bond between nature and himself. Even worse, although he is driven away, the coming of the soldier will not stop the harvest. The earth will not grow infertile, but will continue to bear for the soldier. This is what is hardest to endure: nature is oblivious to human beings; it cares neither for those for whom it provides nor for those it destroys.

To where, asks Meliboeus, will his exile take him?

> Yes, but meanwhile the rest of us are off; some to foregather with the Africans and share their thirst; others to Scythia, and out to where the Oxus rolls the chalk along; others to join the Britons, cut off as they are by the whole width of the world. (lines 64–67)

"At the poem's widest focus, pastoral images have entirely dissolved into images of a nature harsh and strange: parching deserts, the chalky Oaxus [river], remote Britain. To these orderless places the exiles will bear their grief."[17]

To console Meliboeus, Tityrus invites him to postpone his journey and stay for one last night. Offering green leaves for a bed, Tityrus makes it clear that Meliboeus will not have such comfort again.

> Yet surely you could sleep here as my guest for this one night, with green leaves for your bed? I have got ripe apples, and some mealy chestnuts and a good supply of cheese. (lines 79–84)

The consolations offered Meliboeus are material and temporary, lasting only one night. Cheese and apples are poor substitutes for one's own country. Tityrus does not have the power to restore Meliboeus's farm and harvest to him. Above all, he cannot give back the vision Meliboeus had in his pastoral setting, the vision that the world was peaceful and orderly.

This ending to Virgil's poem is not a solution to the problems of the world outside of the ideal pasture. Instead, it is a momentary stay against the chaos out there that Meliboeus will still have to face. "Most literary pastorals do not finally permit us to come away with anything like the simple, affirmative attitude we adopt toward pleasing rural scenery. These works manage to call into question, to qualify, or bring irony to bear against the illusion of peace and harmony in a green pasture. And it is this fact that is the difference between the complex and sentimental kinds of pastoralism."[18]

I shall argue that it is the sentimental version of the pastoral ideal that has been intimately connected with landscape architecture. By using conventions borrowed from the painting of the sixteenth through the twentieth century, the landscape architect has, as we shall see, re-presented the pastoral ideal. Too often, however, such representations have been called natural. By this it is implied that they are representations of a nature that is always good, comfortable, orderly, and peaceful. But as Meliboeus has learned, nature can be powerful, unjust, chaotic, and destructive. To represent nature otherwise is sentimental pastoralism, and designs that do so are obviously not natural. They are fully cultural, with a history all their own.

Meliboeus introduces tension into the poetic vision of the pastoral. He calls into question the ideal of living peacefully and in harmony in a green pasture that recognizes neither the forces of nature nor a potentially threatening society that lies outside its borders. There are sacrilegious soldiers and barbarians out there, and sometimes the she-goat will abandon her offspring. Meliboeus can keep us from feeling too comfortable with a pastoralism that is simply a dream. He can keep us from thinking that nature is a designed pasture or that the pastoral is anything truly natural. Indeed, the pastoral is a bounded, designed refuge from the threats of the city and of nature itself.

If I may speak both anachronistically and metaphorically, Meliboeus is committed to destabilizing the conventions we learn from naturalistic painting and use to design actual places. The familiar image presented by contemporary pastoral designs leaves Meliboeus out. It treats the pastoral as an unambiguously pure and happy vision. But Virgil didn't see things this way. For him, the pastoral ideal was an illusion bounded by a real world that could shatter the rustic peace of the garden.

———

In our brief survey of the Greek theater and Roman painting, we uncovered a host of basic conventions whose influence have been felt throughout the centuries: the singular point of view provided by the theater; the use of the stage screen from which to carve spaces; "screening" to block views; the exterior point of view of illusionary scenes; the interior as seen through doorways; the use of coulisse to frame compositions and give the illusion of greater depth; panoramic and perspective views; and trompe l'oeil. But this list simply enumerates technical aspects of a much larger enterprise: an urban culture's first expression of a growing aesthetic interest in the countryside.

As a result of this interest, influential Romans built their own private parks in the city and painted pictorialized landscapes on the walls of their villas; both are miniaturized versions of "nature." The culmination of all these developments is surely the pastoral landscape embodied by Tityrus. Like a garden it requires faithful maintenance to sustain the appearance of order and control. Yet Tityrus's garden shows no evidence of toil; it gives the appearance of being natural and beautiful. But Meliboeus knows better: an omnipotent and destructive nature could turn it into chaos in a moment.

As we continue, we shall see how these conventions and ideas influence actual landscape design. Before proceeding to that, however, let us briefly look at the Middle Ages, a period when, although the beauty of landscape went largely unrepresented, an important step was taken toward its pictorialization.

4

Cloistering the Spectator:
The Middle Ages

St. Anselm, writing at the beginning of the twelfth century, maintained that things were harmful in proportion to the number of
senses which they delighted, and therefore rated it dangerous to
sit in a garden where there were roses to satisfy the senses of
sight and smell, and songs and stories to please the ears. This,
no doubt, expresses the strictest monastic view. The average lay-
man would not have thought it wrong to enjoy nature; he would
simply have said that nature was not enjoyable.[1]

From Saint Anselm we immediately learn something basic about the
Middle Ages. In contrast to the open and continuous sense of landscape we have just observed in classical depiction, the medieval tendency was to close oneself off from the landscape. The Middle Ages
was a time of turning inward, away from the outside world, away
from observation. Such an attitude would hardly seem conducive to
producing much of interest for an environmental designer. Indeed,
the Middle Ages, spanning the years from about 400 to 1400, are
not noteworthy for developments in pictorial illusion. This does not
mean, however, that they have nothing to teach us. As we shall see, a
singular and important contribution was made during the Middle
Ages: medieval artists followed their classical predecessors by redis-
covering the illusion of unlimited depth. And it is through an expansion of this discovery that Renaissance perspective developed.

Dwindling Observation

Today we have to be reminded that there was a time in which people
would probably have found little amusement in observing the landscape. The sense of detachment and the security necessary to stand
back and look at the landscape appreciatively was simply nonexistent
during the Middle Ages. The pleasures that could be found in nature
had become subordinate to battles for salvation and survival. A walk
in the woods might have been terrifying, the view from a mountain-
top unappreciated. In a frightening and unpleasant wilderness dotted
with castles and churches, there was no desire for broad, unified

views of landscape. If looking at one's surroundings was neither plea-surable nor beneficial, it is not surprising that the paintings of the time disclosed little interest in observation. "The symbols by which early mediaeval art acknowledged the existence of natural objects bore unusually little relation to their actual appearance."[2] This re-veals an attitude toward art very different than that found in natural-ism; it makes no attempt to mirror or to improve upon the visible world.

Medieval artists often depicted natural objects in a way that looks to us as if they were deliberately trying to dispute what they saw with their own eyes. For example, trees were often framed in a dark out-line so that they gave the impression of a single entity—one gigantic leaf or mushroom. As late as the thirteenth century, those who wished to paint mountains were advised to take stones as their models.[3]

The medieval eye refused the unified point of view we have seen in ancient painting; instead, it saw only details. In landscape depiction, this idea was demonstrated in the decorative, rather than naturalistic, disposal of plants and earth forms. Flowers fill the sky like a tapestry, and barren rocks are piled up to act as stages for events in a linear story. The medieval tendency was to picture nature in terms of these identifiable objects rather than in terms of views or scenes.

There were no pastoral views, like those observed in Roman paint-ings, for another reason as well. Hellenistic and Roman landscapes were the product of urban cultures, such as those of Athens, Rome, and Pompeii. Medieval civilization, however, was predominantly rural in the West, and rural conditions tend not to encourage a taste for the pastoral.[4] The rural landscape is not an object of beauty for one who works in its midst, only for one who views it from a distance.

Looking at a view, or a scene, requires that the viewer assume a particular fixed location for viewing, one that rules out other points of view. By contrast, in medieval paintings, mosaics, and manuscript illuminations, things were spread over a surface as though each one were facing the viewer independently. Objects we would expect to see hidden behind one another appear next to each other, or with one above the other. The individual pictorial elements, whether figures, buildings, or landscape features, lose the illusion of three-dimensional form and become two-dimensional shapes. These pictorial techniques suggest a point of view in which objects are not related to each other in space. Like the sculpturally real, they pose an alternative to the familiar perspectival view that for us has been dominant since the Renaissance. Indeed, they challenge the very notion that viewing the landscape across space, as when looking at the prospect offered by a scenic outlook, can be at all gratifying.

Even given everything just stated, it would be a mistake to charac-terize the medieval period simply as a regressive age so far as paint-ing was concerned. There were important ways in which medieval artists did preserve the traditions of their ancient predecessors. Most significantly, they left an opening, an aperture to space, through which the Renaissance would peek out. Despite obvious discontinuities with the past, there is an important sense in which the ancient pictorial conventions remain in continuous use throughout the medieval period.

Pictured Landscape

Medieval artists were essentially copyists, and this is the first and most obvious way in which they maintained some continuity with the ancient world. When they drew, they copied from older pictures rather than relying on their own observations. The principal form of drawing was manuscript illumination: artists would illustrate sacred texts. (For example, see the ninth-century psalter, fig. 4.5) The "original" drawings, compositional rules, and authority upon which the illuminations were based were taken from old Greek manuscripts.[5] The manuscript illuminators always had before them copies—many times removed—of original Greek works.

In the depiction of landscape the artist-as-copyist had to follow strict rules. Perhaps the most striking convention of the Middle Ages is the "broken terrace." This rocky landscape was a feature of backgrounds from early classical times to the fifteenth century, and for long periods it was the only distinct tradition in landscape painting.[6] It is a good example of how pictorial techniques become firmly established conventions.

The rocky terrain of the Odyssey Landscapes (fig. 4.1) may have been based on actual observation of the Apennine mountains behind Rome and Naples. The ancient painters may actually have been trying to represent what they saw in the landscape. In outcrops, even today, a bedded structure of limestone in horizontal strata is visible, with jointing along lines of weakness forming quadrangular blocks.[7] But the medievalists were not looking to actual mountains as models. They were copying from pictures. The result is that a stylized version of the Apennines became the convention for depicting all mountains. In a wall mosaic (fig. 4.4) constructed five hundred years after the first-century Odyssey Landscapes, we can see the blocky structure that was used to represent mountains. Even in some Renaissance paintings of the fifteenth century (fig. 4.2), painted some one thousand years later, this convention was still used to create mountains rising to fantastic heights. The more mountains were copied from ancient models, the more they became independent of local geology and vegetation.

Why would such a stylized (and not very convincing) version of mountains be copied for so long? First, because actual mountains

Fig. 4.1. *The Arrival of Ulysses in the Land of the Laestrygonians* (detail). Museo Profano, Vatican. (Alinari/Art Resource, New York.)

were not revered as much as ancient representations of them were. More importantly, the imitation of this rocky structure was a painter's delight. The effect of rock terraces solved many of the problems of spatial representation for medieval painters. The sharply defined verticals and horizontals gave obvious opportunities for shading contrasts. They also provided the opportunity to portray a narrative path that had much in common with a medieval play; in other words, it was like a processional that trailed through the streets. Without obscuring any of the characters, trees and other foreground elements stood as independent symbols to support the story line rather than to ensure the picture's faithfulness to actual views. Finally, the "broken terrace" became a kind of shorthand, easy to draw but readily recognizable as mountains.

The extraordinary continuity of this convention was superseded only by the local realism of fifteenth-century Flemish landscape painting and—ironically—Italian painting of the very landscape that had inspired the "broken terrace" convention. The detail of a fifteenth-century painting shown in figure 4.3 is in stark contrast to the painting's medieval predecessors; its blending of rock into soil formation shows a concern for the relation of surface to core, a visual inquiry into geology.

The tradition of medieval copying is a prime example of the pictorialization of the landscape. An object was first observed in the landscape, was then depicted conventionally, and was finally copied for so long that as its true origin became forgotten, its conventional de-

Fig. 4.2. Benozzo Gozzoli, *Journey of the Magi* (detail, 1459). Medici Riccardi, Florence. (Alinari/Art Resource, New York.)

Fig. 4.3. Konrad Witz, *Miraculous Draught of the Fishes* (detail, 1444). Genf Museum, Geneva. (Foto Marburg/Art Resource, New York.)

piction was all that remained. The depiction became distorted and stylized, a reflection of pictures rather than of the world. It may be hard to believe that pictures were so powerful that their copies would obliterate their original sources. Or it may seem that this idea of taking pictures for reality is only the product of a cloistered medieval mind—but it isn't: we in the twentieth century do exactly the same thing. Today we see stylized versions of the landscape garden in parks and corporate headquarters that have been copied from earlier gardens that were themselves copied from paintings made three hundred years ago.

Preserving Stage Space

An example of the discontinuity of medieval traditions with ancient ones is the tendency to close the vista formerly framed by coulisse. This can be seen in a picture from the early Middle Ages, a Byzantine mosaic from the sixth century (fig. 4.4). "Especially remarkable is a work such as the Abraham mosaic in San Vitale at Ravenna [Italy] for here we can manifestly establish the disintegration of the perspective idea: not only the vegetation but even the contours of the earth (in the Odyssey Landscapes cut by the edge of the picture as by a window frame) must now adapt themselves to its curve."[8] The picture plane gives little illusion of depth behind its frame, as, for example, a window would. Space is now bounded by its frame, which is not to be looked through but to be filled. This is in striking contrast to the Odyssey Landscapes, whose picture planes gave the impression of more landscape to the sides and beyond.

Despite its lack of perspective depth, this mosaic again reveals some continuity with Hellenistic traditions. For instance, we see suggestions of sky in dotted blue mosaic, hints of perspective in the table, and the ever-present Alexandrian tree. But this continuity is expressed most articulately by the way the mosaic, in its structure, echoes a stage. Curtains and small vertical buildings, almost like niches or side houses, suggest a stage set. In this mosaic, however, there is only a remnant of a side house to make space appear only as deep as a platform. The arched mosaic frame functions much like the ancient stage screen (and like a precursor to the proscenium stage), with a large doorway opening into a scene that is only slightly deeper than the wall. A mountainous landscape is depicted with the broken-terrace convention; now stylized, it proliferates fantastically, and even slopes to fit the curvature of the frame.

This "stage space" structure can be found in Roman scenes where, for example, a garden or a series of figures appears to reside on a narrow ledge. "Stage space" is evident in the division of ground: a horizontal ground plane is placed in front of the background. Instead

Fig. 4.4. *Abraham and the Three Angels* and *Sacrifice of Isaac* (526–46). San Vitale, Ravenna, Italy. (Alinari/Art Resource, New York.)

of standing within the ground plane, figures are supported on its upper contour. No matter how little depth is depicted, this juxtaposition of narrow ground plane and wider background remained throughout the Middle Ages. Despite being largely an art of the surface, this one measure of depth did preserve, did keep in readiness, the ingredients of the ancient perspective construction of space.

Flattening the View

In parts of Europe north of Italy during the ninth century, conventions from ancient landscape depiction were also preserved. The great masterpiece of the Reims School, and one of the most miraculous productions of the Middle Ages, is a psalter from Utrecht, France. The psalter is a collection of psalms or sacred poems which was produced and reproduced many times. In the Utrecht Psalter (fig. 4.5), circa 830, the plain brown line drawings that illustrate the

Fig. 4.5. Utrecht Psalter, illustration for psalm 6 (c. 830). MS. 32, Bibliotheek der Rijksuniversiteit, Utrecht.

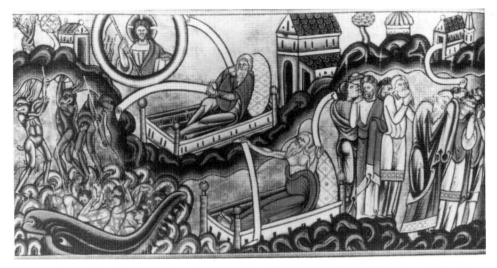

Fig. 4.6. Paris Psalter, illustration for psalm 6 (c. 1200). MS. lat 8846, fol. IIv, Bibliothèque Nationale, Paris.

poems fall into a class by themselves; for they represent the landscape with extraordinary expressiveness. The flair with which the trees, hills, and water are drawn confirm the artist's enthusiasm for landscape forms. The topography rolls as if in the midst of an earthquake, opening up space and reminding us of the classical pastoral paintings, the Odyssey Landscapes.

The Utrecht Psalter is unique because, having been reproduced over centuries, it provides in and of itself a case study for a history of landscape depiction. Across four centuries, we can vividly see movement away from spatial illusion. There is no clearer way to show the progressive flattening of the view than to compare, for example, psalm 6 from both the ninth and thirteenth centuries (figs. 4.5 and 4.6).[9]

The later drawing is framed, and the figures are frozen. Landscape, composed of mountains and water, is conventionalized and reduced to a regular curly outline. Impressionistic trees, composed of figure and void in the earlier drawing, have become stylized and decorative, resembling flowers or mushrooms wrought in metal. Comparing the two drawings is like comparing a landscape garden from the middle of the eighteenth century with one from the middle of the twentieth: in the latter, conventions have hardened into dogmatic forms that lack the freshness that "irregular" landscape design once had before it became conventionalized.

The use of coulisse, in this case hills set "behind" one another, provides spatial continuity in the earlier drawing. In the second drawing, rather than suggesting depth, landforms merely divide the picture space into a series of independently contrived scenes. What shows itself clearly in the later copy of the Utrecht Psalter is the final disappearance of the methods of representing spatial relations that had been achieved in antiquity. Now line provides an emphatic boundary to shapes, and ornaments the surface without suggesting depth; surface is merely surface, no longer giving the illusion of space.

Reclaiming Space

Once again, however, it would be a mistake to read such flattening of illusionary space as indicating that drawing had completely ceased to progress, for even here a significant step was taken toward the perspective construction of the Renaissance. As Panofsky has pointed out, there is a great irony in the flattening of spatial illusion: it is actually the precondition for the truly modern representation of space.[10] His argument? In abandoning perspective depth, medievals returned both objects and space to the picture plane. By doing this, they essentially unified objects and space, and the fate of one became the fate of the other. When objects finally were freed from the pictorial surface (which happened during the Renaissance), space had to go along with them. Deep views of landscape, which depend on the spatial recession of linear perspective, were thus made possible. According to Panofsky, the first step of this process, this emancipation of space, occurred in thirteenth-century France.

The rebirth of both objects and space is best exemplified in the sculptural members of the Gothic cathedral of the High Middle Ages (fig. 4.7). Though they are sculpture, they are one of the first contributions to Renaissance perspective. These Gothic statues stand in a space that is defined by a baldachin, a canopy that defines an outdoor "room," inherited from the earliest stages and paintings. Look again at the Greek vase illustrating scenes from the ancient play *Medea* (fig. 3.2). The central pavilion provides an outdoor room in which the

Fig. 4.7. Reims Cathedral (facade detail, 1225–90). (Foto Marburg/Art Resource, New York.)

body of the dead bride lies. Now reconsider figure 4.7 and notice how the shadow-casting "pavilion" of the cathedral's baldachin fulfills the same function as the pavilion of ancient theater: it provides the figures, now freed from a planar surface, with their own outdoor room.

There is a great difference, however, between the central pavilion of the ancient theater and the baldachins of the Gothic cathedral. In the cathedral, the sculpted room is repeated for each statue. It is this very repetition of space, once it is recessed into the distance, that became the basis for Renaissance perspective. The central pavilion floated aimlessly in space, whereas not only do the baldachins form "rooms" around each statue but their location within the portal gives the appearance of diminution. It does not seem accidental that they form an opening, doorways to the interior of the cathedral. When the techniques of repetition and diminution were first translated into painting, such an opening exposed interior space. But quickly thereafter, the aperture revealed exterior space and exposed our primary interest—the landscape.

The Cloistered Garden

Medieval illustrations offer an alternative to naturalistic scenes. They do not reflect the visible world, nor do they try to convince us they are a believable likeness. Quite like these pictures, the cloistered gardens of the Middle Ages also resisted the temptation of the outside world. They too turned inward, away from landscape.

With the collapse of the western Roman Empire at the beginning of the Middle Ages, garden art dwindled to such an extent that we may say, without exaggerating its loss, that it virtually disappeared. During the late Middle Ages, however, at about the same time that the Gothic cathedral was reclaiming space, the garden began its return to Western life. Twelfth-century gardens were square, enclosed, and, like all art of the Middle Ages, symbolic: "A garden enclosed is my sister, my spouse; a spring shut up, a fountain sealed."[11] In religious houses a walled garden was the symbolic environment of the Virgin Mary.

Some fourteenth-century paintings of gardens reveal a typical manner of depicting plants: they are decoratively dispersed about the surface of the painting as they would be in a tapestry or as mountains would be in the "broken-terrace" convention. Such gardens look as though plants have been stacked upon one another, or resemble gardens observed from an aerial position. This pictorial device allows the spectator to see a display of flowers, each individually, without foreground obstructions. Such a technique communicates the detail and delicacy of a sensuous experience, yet since it is not an eye-level view it seems as if it is of another world.

Enclosed, inwardly oriented, square gardens dramatically parallel the developments we have seen occurring in pictures during this period. The atmospheric distances and city vistas of Roman painting and the outward, spatial connections to the landscape of Greek site planning are, in both the paintings and gardens of the Middle Ages, turned inward, enclosed, and flattened. Medieval gardens set themselves apart from the world that lay just outside, choosing not to look at distant prospects of landscape.

———

We have looked at a few highlights of the thousand years during which the depiction of space became increasingly flat. Despite this flattening, however, we have seen "stage space," actually inherited from the ancient theater, preserved in pictures. In the cathedral we saw not only stage space but also the introduction of the concept of the unlimited extension of space. It is precisely upon this idea that Renaissance artists based their construction of the deep perspective views that we shall investigate next.

Centering the Spectator: The Renaissance

5

In this chapter we shall consider what is perhaps the most decisive period, as well as the most powerful pictorial convention, in the history of landscape depiction: the Renaissance and its development of linear perspective. Landscape itself, however, was not initially a principal subject of pictures during this time. Instead, it was present only as a background to other, more primary, subjects. To this background the spectator's gaze was inexorably led by the mathematical rigor of linear perspective, and it was here that the landscape as we conceive of it today began to take form.

Foreground Perspective Leads to Landscape Background

The development of linear perspective was the essential condition that made possible the expansion of landscape backgrounds. Linear perspective extended the vanishing point out into space and thereby extended into deep vistas of broad landscape the "stage space" we have already seen in pictures. To illustrate this crucial development, I shall concentrate on a series of pictures depicting a single subject: the Christian theme of the Annunciation.[1] By restricting our view to this one subject we shall better be able to pinpoint the specific techniques that were developed to depict the landscape. To summarize in advance, the earliest portrayals of the Annunciation used the stage screen and stage space inherited, respectively, from the ancient stage and from medieval painting. The later works manifest the development of linear perspective in their use of a central, one-point, eye-level viewing position. When this occurred a breakthrough had been reached: a tool had been discovered to pictorialize the deep space necessary for landscapes.[2]

It was in northern Italy, at the beginning of the fourteenth century, that the Byzantine and Gothic pasts met to give rise to perspective. The one person traditionally associated with this great development is Giotto. Indeed, Giotto revolutionized art in Italy and the entire Western world. Yet when we look at one of the first pictures he painted, the *Annunciation* (fig. 5.1), we find that it looks like a stage

Fig. 5.1. Giotto, *Annunciation* (1305). Scrovegni Chapel, Padua. (Alinari/Art Resource, New York.)

set. Curtains are tied open to frame and give depth to interiors. In fact our eyes do not deceive us here, since the buildings he depicted are actually derived "from constructions used in the dramatizations of the Annunciation that actually took place during the Trecento in Padua."[3] Because those plays were staged outside in the streets, we see in the painting the facades of buildings, with openings that lead "inside." Giotto succeeds in giving the viewer a pictorial experience once limited to seated spectators of ancient plays: the experience of being outside and looking into the contained space of a room.

Giotto's "stage set" was a pair of frescoes painted inside a chapel; the figures kneel inside another building which, on Mary's side, Giotto boldly flooded with light. Though the frescoes represent interiors, their backgrounds were painted blue not only to symbolize Heaven but also to conform to the convention of the outdoor stage. The Italian word *cielo,* used to designate the interior vaults of such a building, actually means "sky." Indeed, for centuries theater interiors (and even some modern movie theaters) have had ceilings painted like the sky, some with stars and clouds. These painted skies inside buildings help us to recall the ancient Greek theater, which was outside and had the actual landscape in view. This atavistic convention of bringing the outdoors inside demonstrates one of many ways in which painting has depended upon ancient stage design, which itself was first conceived in the landscape.

Giotto introduced landscapes only when the theme required them or when they produced a dramatic effect in his painting. For example, it was Giotto who first saw the decorative effect of a switchback trail, trodden by groups of people, passing through a hilly landscape (fig. 4.2). This convention was then used for hundreds of years to tell stories in pictures, according to the same conventions that directed medieval processional plays along the streets.

In Giotto's painting only the side houses were constructed with perspective lines. It was Ambrogio Lorenzetti who first took the important step of also using perspective lines to construct the floor.[4] What makes a picture like Lorenzetti's *Annunciation* (fig. 5.2) so significant is the fact that here for the first time the ground plane is no longer the shallow floor of a stage severed by the edges of the picture. Instead, it is the bottom surface of a strip of space which can be thought of as stretching on either side to any distance. The floor now actually extends under the figures and thereby becomes an index of dimensions, for figure and ground alike. We can measure the floors by counting the squares, and Panofsky suggests that it is not going too far to assert that such a pattern is the first example of a coordinate system, illustrated in art before it had been postulated by abstract mathematical thought.[5] Today this very coordinate system has been applied to the ground plane of most of the United States.

An overwhelming fact of linear perspective is that the picture space

Fig. 5.2. Ambrogio Lorenzetti, *Annunciation* (1344). (Alinari/Art Resource, New York.)

becomes an extension of the viewer's space. The lines of Lorenzetti's floor pattern allow the viewer the illusion of entering the picture, providing lines of approach and movement. Lorenzetti's floor succeeds in presenting the illusion that the figures themselves are surrounded by space. The front of the floor ends abruptly, however, still suggesting that the figures are on stage and that, as spectators, we are in the audience. The front face of the vaults and the line where the floor drops off form the picture plane, which in this case determines the boundaries between inside and out.

Yet we are not quite sure who is in and who is out. The reason for our confusion is that, in the rear, the floor is bounded neither by the interior wall of a room nor by the landscape. Instead, it is bounded by a gold background traditionally used in many paintings of the Middle Ages. Gold symbolized heaven and tells us that this announcement is not occurring in any place we know, or even in the same world we inhabit. Nevertheless, the active perspective lines of Lorenzetti's floor puncture and replace the symbolic gold background and thus make space for naturalistic landscape views that are to be seen in later paintings.

Legitimate linear perspective construction was demonstrated in 1420 by the architect Brunelleschi and was later formulated in writing by Alberti in his 1511 book *On Painting*.[6] In his treatise, Alberti was the first to describe a painting as a window through which we look at the visible world. With this idea of the picture plane as window, the Renaissance had arrived at a notion that would inform the basis of naturalistic painting and, consequently, our habits of seeing both pictures and the visible world.

In Filippo Lippi's *Annunciation* (fig. 5.3), one-point, eye-level perspective is fully illustrated. In place of the gold or blue backgrounds seen in the previous two paintings, a landscape has appeared.[7] Gabriel has entered the space of an open loggia in which Mary hesitantly has placed one foot. Compared to the two previous Annunciations, Mary's figure is quite changed. She is facing us, the viewers, almost frontally. As a result, she induces our participation in the picture. An angel gazes over his shoulder at the spectator as if to acknowledge our presence. These figures confirm the powerful, direct, eye-level relationship between spectators and paintings constructed using linear perspective. We do not yet occupy the figures' space, however, for we are still essentially in the audience of the theater, separated by elaborate architectural framing devices. Nevertheless, we can now see deep into the distance.

Beyond Mary and Gabriel, stylized trees occupy the deep perspective of a city garden. Though it looks much more like an actual place than do the gold or blue backgrounds of earlier Annunciations, it is nevertheless not meant to represent one; its primary function is to symbolize the Virgin's chastity. (Not only did paintings of gardens symbolize the constraints placed upon Mary's behavior, but actual gardens separated women from the public world.)

In Leonardo da Vinci's *Annunciation* (fig. 5.4), we see an evocation of landscape that practically appears modern. Gabriel and Mary are now outdoors. Though their clothes (which are traditional for the period) and particularly Gabriel's wings give them away, the rest of

Fig. 5.3. Filippo Lippi, *Annunciation* (c. 1440). Lorenzo, Florence. (Alinari/Art Resource, New York.)

the picture looks as though it might even be a modern representation of an actual place. But that is only because we recognize period clothes more easily than period landscapes. The spectators of this painting were used to reading narrative in landscape paintings and would have known that the Annunciation panel was not intended to depict a place familiar to the painter. (Moreover, they cared little about depictions of real places.)

This seemingly naturalistic landscape is, in fact, composed of elements that are primarily symbolic and support the traditional narrative that locates the event in Nazareth. The four flamelike trees screening the event are cypress trees, which symbolize Mary's lofty contemplation. The other trees look like pines and cedars, which are associated with Mount Sion, a place connected symbolically with Mary. They are easily recognized as symbols because they look rather like single leaves sitting awkwardly on the top of the wall, quite out of scale with the landscape background.

However, one aspect of the painting which contributes to its modernity is the fact that Leonardo's concise depiction omits many of the traditional symbols. Unlike Lippi's *Annunciation* (fig. 5.3), for exam-

Fig. 5.4. Leonardo da Vinci, *Annunciation* (late 1470s). (Alinari/Art Resource, New York.)

ple; it does not include God the Father, auxiliary angels, the Dove of the Holy Spirit, or biblical, allegorical, or saintly figures. Mary is seated on a protected threshold adjoining a splendid villa. Gabriel kneels before her on a rich carpet of grass and flowers holding a lily, universally associated with the Annunciation. The remaining flora are invented, but together they associate the Annunciation with spring, specifically, of course, with March 25.

This flowering field is not a native meadow that Leonardo painted on site or from memory. Instead, it is what is traditionally called the *hortus conclusus,* an "enclosed garden" symbolizing Mary's virginity. This description of the garden, however, is misleading, for it is neither physically nor visually enclosed. The parapet wall is lower even than the eye level of a seated person, and it is pierced by an opening that leads to a road winding through a distant landscape.

Behind Gabriel the landscape is populated with neither people nor structures, while behind Mary the landscape is bustling with activity. Gabriel's landscape might refer to an earthly paradise and Mary's to her role as protector of humanity. "In the sky to the left above Gabriel, the sun breaks through some clouds. It appears perfectly natural, yet is a simple, disguised symbol used by Leonardo for the descent of the Word."[8]

The depiction of distance is enhanced by a hazy atmosphere that extends to a faraway coast and a minutely depicted harbor town, complete with a lighthouse and sailing vessels. The harbor is an unconventional addition by Leonardo symbolizing a refuge for sinners in the sea of the world.[9] Harbors had not been related visually to Annunciation scenes before this but appeared in them with some frequency afterward.

Located precisely at the central vanishing point of the perspective is a fog-covered mountain dominating the harbor. Like the pines and cedars mentioned above, it, too, might represent Mount Sion. In this early work, Leonardo had accepted the convention of drawing mountains using rocks as models. Later, however, he contributed to the upheaval of attitudes about the formation of mountains with a scientific account that included studies of geological strata to show the forces that led to their formation. Early Renaissance perspectives such as Leonardo's stand as a transition between the symbolic and the naturalistic. Without knowledge of the meanings of the symbols, a viewer might be convinced that Leonardo was trying to depict a place familiar to him.

In the Annunciation panel by Lorenzo di Credi painted at the end of the fifteenth century (fig. 5.5), Mary and Gabriel are indoors again. The floor of the interior space continues, illusorily, underneath the feet of the spectator. We, too, are indoors, and the vanishing point of linear perspective leads us to a distant horizon. Our line of sight is through an open doorway leading to a landscape that is now literally outdoors. Since the end of the fifteenth century, we have gained a better understanding of what the word *outdoors* really means. Perspective devices today habitually lead our eyesight through doors, windows, picture frames, and camera lenses to landscapes beyond.

The point of view represented in di Credi's work radically reverses that found in the ancient theater. There, the spectator was sitting outside looking through arched openings to interiors. In the transformation from the stage to painting, the spectator has moved inside and the landscape is outdoors. The landscape is now scenery that is seen from the secure and comfortable point of view of a spectator who is indoors.

Such a view does not seem surprising to us. We expect the landscape to be outdoors, and indeed anything else would seem unnatural to us. But where did these doors come from? The Renaissance view of the landscape, in whose shadow we still stand today, is a consequence of a specific artistic device that, when it becomes pervasive, has enormous implications: continually looking out at the landscape from inside eventually makes one accustomed to being separated from it, to being sheltered and comforted when viewing it, to seeing it pictorially. This interior point of view can be maintained even if one actually *is* outside with only a camera serving as the window, or it can be maintained just with the memory of how those pictorial framing conventions have served as the window between the spectator and the view.

Although perspective led Renaissance artists to create distant, convincing illusions of landscapes, we must keep reminding ourselves that these landscapes are not intended to represent actual places. The prominence of the landscape upon which di Credi's composition is

Fig. 5.5. Lorenzo di Credi, *Annunciation* (late fifteenth century). (Alinari/Art Resource, New York.)

centered might lead us to think that landscape is the central idea. Not so. In fact, it is the three openings themselves that are the central symbols. Only incidentally, and in conjunction with the idea of Mary's garden, does the doorway focus on the landscape. Awkward views of distant, pastoral landscapes appear through windows. Yet these neat clumps of trees with irregular but carefully contrived sight lines surely must make us look ahead to the eighteenth century. As we shall see shortly, Capability Brown's work depended on just such pictorial conventions.

In our brief survey of depictions of the Annunciation we have seen the development of linear perspective, which placed its vanishing point in the landscape. From the Renaissance on, it is safe to say that the viewpoint of the spectator has remained, figuratively, inside the window of Renaissance perspective—whether the landscape is viewed through actual windows, doors, picture planes, or camera lenses. Even our language confirms that we still see the landscape as "outdoors." The desire to see a distant landscape from a comfortable and secure position, buffered by a hefty space, continues to be a powerful force that reverberates throughout our relationship with the landscape. Above all, these paintings acknowledge the location of spectators in relation to "scenery" in a way that provides both a singular point of view and a centered one. As a result, the empowerment of the spectator is a profound legacy of the projection of the vanishing point into the distance by the technique of linear perspective, because the depiction of distance between the horizon and the spectator provides the security of shelter and the feeling of control. The landscapes we have seen in these Annunciations were symbolic; still, their vanishing point has led to a distant and naturalistic horizon.

Perspective in Practice

It is striking and a reflection of a basic scenic habit that, like the paintings we have discussed, actual Renaissance gardens used framing devices to set off views of distant landscapes. As a matter of fact, Renaissance innovation in garden design occurred not within gardens but in the relationship of gardens to the larger landscape.[10] In Renaissance Italy, the thin, crenellated wall of the medieval garden became a wide structure of loggias, rooms, and paths on different levels, each leading the eye of the stroller outward to the distant landscape. This is precisely the technique found in the Lippi *Annunciation* (fig. 5.3), or in da Vinci's use of lowered walls in his *Annunciation* (fig. 5.4). Just as deep vistas began to appear in painting, so too the medieval garden wall was punctured and opened up to an expansive and perspectival view (fig. 5.6). In short, gardens, which typically have been considered the primary source for the history of landscape architecture, are themselves repositories of images formulated by painters, even though those images were never intended to represent actual places.

Alberti's expertise in producing illusory views also informs his advice for the siting of villas: "They should not be set in the most fertile part of the fields but on the summit of a hill, or on a height, which would afford the possibility of a panorama of 360 degrees."[11] One of the earliest gardens to be focused on the surrounding landscape, and

Fig. 5.6. Palazzo Piccolomini garden (after 1460), Pienza, Italy. (Copyright 1987 Mary Sayer Hammond.)

indeed the one that has remained relatively unchanged, is in the Palazzo Piccolomini in Pienza. It was designed in 1460 by Bernardo Rossellino, a student of Alberti's, and its designer's intention to take advantage of the view is clear in this passage written by its patron, Pius II:

> Looking from the highest room toward the West, (one) sees beyond Ilcino and Siena, and even as far as the Alps of Pistoia. On the North, the landscape offers a variety of hills with their gay and verdant woods, spreading widely five thousand *passi;* a sharp eye can also see the Apennines, but the depth of the river Chiana makes it impossible to see Cortona, the town settled upon that high hill not far from the lake of Trasimeno, which looks over the valley situated in between.[12]

The visual integration of the wide panorama with the garden, in the manner described in detail by Pius II, had a profound effect not only on the design of gardens but also on attitudes toward the very look of the landscape. When this process of employing painterly conventions in the design of gardens reached its zenith in the eighteenth century, the result can be expressed reversibly: the garden as a landscape, the landscape as garden. In short, by the eighteenth century the entire landscape was considered to be within the purview of design.

Very dramatic perspectival conventions leaped from painting to plazas such as Saint Peter's in Rome, designed by Bernini in 1656. There a pedestrian can observe the columns of the elliptical colonade in perfect alignment. A false perspective brings the facade of Saint Peter's somewhat forward to the approaching observer and, conversely, increases the apparent distance to the obelisk. The perspectival power of the facade, its vanishing point terminating uncompromisingly at the central door and window, is heightened by the elevated slope of the entire plaza and still more by the extraordinary lift spectators feel by the monumental steps. Walking up these steps, the pedestrian sees the statues of the saints rise into the sky.

Sixteenth-century French travelers were drawn to Italy by engraved pictures of such gardens and piazzas. Consequently, former French medieval castle gardens that had been enclosed, inwardly oriented, and defensive in spirit gradually took on Italian habits. In other words, the French borrowed the conventions and perspectival techniques the Italians had inherited from painters. By the seventeenth century the French would employ these techniques to an unparalleled degree: they would extend the view from actual gardens all the way to the horizon. At Versailles, for example, all five miles from Louis's balcony to the skyline was commissioned for design.

Theater productions in seventeenth-century gardens would also take advantage of the principles of perspective. The interior of a theater in Versailles, for example, was constructed out of trees and hedges to frame the stage, whose background was the actual garden. Further, entire gardens became part of a theatrical experience through the use of painted and actual garden perspectives that exploited the limitless possibilities of the surroundings. Radiating walks were incorporated into the staging. The length and width of allées and walks were manipulated to dramatize perspective, and large sheets of water were used to form optical distortions.[13]

———

Alberti was the first to say that paintings are like windows to the world. With the examples discussed in this chapter we have seen how our vision of the world can be fundamentally informed by the conventions of paintings.

The pictorial construction of "stage space" in Giotto's painting of the *Annunciation*, gave the spectator, who was inside a building, the pictorial illusion of being outside looking in. A later painting of the Annunciation gave the illusion of being comfortably inside looking out. The security of looking out at the landscape, through a window, anticipates the pleasure of seeing landscape as the primary subject in later paintings.

While these portrayals of the Annunciation manifest hardly anything about "nature" in the sense we are used to, they reveal a great deal about naturalism: we have seen the landscape in painting, even if symbolically, change from a gold background to a scene that looks much like the world with which we are familiar. Even further, through our brief look at Renaissance gardens we have learned a good deal more about our central role not only as spectators but also as pedestrians in actual places designed with perspective in mind. Next we shall walk right up to one of those openings provided by perspective and look out at a landscape panorama.

6

Elevating the Spectator: The Renaissance

Accurate linear perspective, largely restricted to the construction of the foreground in previous examples, produced landscapes that served as scenic backdrops behind windows or doorways. There was at the same time, however, a growing desire for more: for deep and continuous views of landscape. This led to the development of another significant pictorial convention, the panorama. In the works that follow, we shall see how panoramic landscapes were viewed from elevated, foreground viewing positions.

Though according to the *Oxford English Dictionary* the word *panorama* did not appear in English until late in the eighteenth century,[1] it has roots in antiquity. The two Greek roots of the word mean "all" and "see," and as we ourselves shall see, panoramic paintings attempt to depict a comprehensive view of landscape. The technique of spatial recession, which provides the illusion of greater distances by the diminution of objects, was prefigured in the Roman Odyssey Landscapes (fig. 3.4). Throughout the Middle Ages, however, such an extensive view of the landscape was largely absent.

Panoramic painting reemerged fully in the fifteenth century and attempted to represent a comprehensive view of a subject, typically a landscape. In the paintings we shall look at now, this extensive view was achieved by using an aerial viewpoint (a vantage point unusual in the Renaissance). Though this approach provides a more extensive view of landscape than any we have seen so far, the landscape is still most often spread out behind a primary subject.

The First Recorded Prospect

In the fourteenth century the poet Petrarch saw the landscape from an aerial viewpoint. He was not quite as comfortable looking at distant landscapes as we are today. As the story is frequently told, he was the first person to climb a mountain to enjoy the view from the top. When he arrived and gazed across the distant prospect of the Alps, he said, "I was abashed, . . . angry with myself that I should still be admiring earthly things."[2] This story reveals a conflict in Petrarch's attitude: he was at once a true medieval as well as a harbinger of the modern desire to appreciate and take pleasure in the landscape. His desire to enjoy a view, a desire once rare and even threatening, is now commonplace. As we shall see, five centuries of landscape painting were extremely important in effecting this change.

Though Petrarch thrived in the city, he described in great detail the farm where he lived and his rocky retreats. "He was probably the first man to express the emotion on which the existence of landscape painting [and landscape architecture] so largely depends: the desire to escape from the turmoil of cities into the peace of the countryside."[3] Here again is the classic pastoral ideal, revived by Petrarch, translated into painting and later, as we shall see, into landscape design as well.

Panoramic Elevation

One of the most sensitive panoramas ever painted was created during Petrarch's lifetime. Ambrogio Lorenzetti, whose *Annunciation* we have already seen (fig. 5.2), painted *The Good Government in the Country* (fig. 6.1) in the Palazzo Pubblico in Siena, which overlooks the famous Piazza del Campo. In Lorenzetti's frescoes, we see the rarely depicted theme of the interdependence of the city and the countryside: both are happy when good government reigns.

Since ancient times, small representations of hills, and occasionally buildings, had been drawn in elevation against and within the plan view of maps.[4] From these maps developed the panoramic, or bird's-eye, perspective. Lorenzetti's painting is somewhere between a picture-map and a bird's-eye view. Painters such as Lorenzetti had no airplanes or satellites from which they could take photographs: at best Lorenzetti would have looked out of the second-story window of the Palazzo Pubblico, where he was painting, to observe the Sienese countryside.

In *The Good Government in the Country,* we can see the details of flowers, trees, cultivated fields, and scenes of peasant and courtly activity. Although it is an idealized illustration of the ordered life of the countryside, and there is much that is awkward in the perspective, the illusion of its portrayal of an actual location is extraordinary for its time. The landscape of Tuscany, where it was painted, is composed of small hills and valleys with native ilex and cypress, interspersed with small farm buildings and irregular field patterns of olive trees and grapevines. Lorenzetti's panoramas of Siena and the surrounding countryside are "the first postclassical vistas essentially derived from visual experience rather than from tradition, memory and imagination."[5] Pictures such as this one would inspire others to seek actual panoramic views of the landscape.

These frescoes are not yet based on linear perspective, in which the composition would be sucked in toward a single point opposite the spectator. Instead, all visual relationships in the painting are dependent on the city rather than on the spectator who is viewing the scene. The countryside is an extension of the city's space; castles, houses, and bridges are all seen from the direction of the city. Even light originates from the city.[6] In addition, all the features of the countryside diminish in proportion to their distance from the city, not in proportion to their distance from the spectator of the painting. The city in this painting is the forerunner of today's spectator, always looking out from itself—the center of the world.

Terrace Landscapes

Because Lorenzetti's painting had no foreground subject, Lorenzetti was spared a problem that most fifteenth-century Italian and Dutch painters had to face: how to unite the foreground subject with the panorama. There were two solutions. The first was to place foreground figures (suitably religious or noble) on a plateau or elevated

Fig. 6.1. Ambrogio Lorenzetti, *The Good Government in the Country* (1338–39). Palazzo Publico, Siena. (Alinari/Art Resource, New York.)

terrace that dropped away to the broad landscape below. The second was to let the foreground subjects simply float out in space above a distant landscape panorama.

A good example of the terrace solution is *The Madonna and Chancellor Rolin* by Jan van Eyck (fig. 6.2). Through three openings we see a panoramic landscape: a busy town, densely packed buildings, a winding river, a bridge, thousands of people, and snowy mountains in the distance. The motif of a view up a river valley, with hills dipping to the water's edge and the minute details of a distant town, is a standard Renaissance convention. These hills placed in front of one another use the stage technique of coulisse to depict the

Fig. 6.2. Jan van Eyck, *The Madonna and Chancellor Rolin* (1425). Musée du Louvre, Paris.

river corridor. The river valley motif is a notable achievement: the representation of distance provided by the river valley is considerably more convincing than the coulisse of overlapping hills we observed in the Middle Ages.

Portrayals of distant views from high terraces proliferated not only because of beautiful examples such as van Eyck's but also because making such pictures solves some compositional problems for the painter: it offers the closest approximation in landscape to the artificial conditions of one-point perspective. Once a ground plane was established, river banks converged like the coulisses of a stage set, regularly overlapping each other as they diminished in size in orderly fashion. The use of the terrace convention implies that the type of landscape the artist chose to represent may have resulted more from the mechanics of composition than from the appreciation of particular landscape features such as, in this case, river valleys.

Portrait Landscapes

The second solution for the problems involved in creating a panorama was to locate the panorama behind a portrait. (Portraiture had itself been reinvented in the fourteenth century.) During the Middle Ages, instead of trying to represent their subjects realistically, portrait artists had produced conventional figures of a man or a woman, simply writing on each portrait the name of the person it was intended to represent. At the same time that artists were beginning to draw landscapes to look like ones that actually existed, likenesses of people were also being depicted.[7]

Portraits were typically painted against immense landscape panoramas illustrating the earthly status of the people painted. The landscape sits well below Piero della Francesca's portraits *Battista Sforza* and *Federigo da Montefeltro* (fig. 6.3). What better way to illustrate an attitude of dominance than through the use of this convention? We still design with it today when we construct scenic lookouts from towers, bridges, highways, monuments, and buildings.

Piero, a friend of Alberti, was the greatest living master of perspective. The hilly topography behind these portraits diminishes into the distance at a convincing rate. The warm olive browns of the foreground gradually become light, cool blues at the horizon, suggesting an atmospheric perspective that mingles with the clouds. The city represented in the background of *Battista Sforza* is identifiable as Borgo San Sepolcro, but the landscapes are contrived to serve another purpose: "Piero was in touch with the major intellectual and scientific currents of his time, and must have known his Tuscan contemporary Paolo del Pozzo Toscanelli, who believed the world was round (and made the map that started Columbus on his voyage).

Fig. 6.3. Piero della Francesca, *Battista Sforza* and *Federigo da Montefeltro* (after 1474). (Alinari/Art Resource, New York.)

Piero set out to prove this proposition visually, by establishing a continuous plain of a kind rarely to be found in Italy."[8] Consequently, the hills that rise from the plain do not do so in ranges as they actually do in Tuscany. Instead, they form independent knobs that diminish into the distance at a rate that demonstrates that the landscape is the surface of a sphere. To further convey this scientific thesis, the plain's surface is slightly curved.

This picture of a landscape illustrates some features of an actual place, a town in Italy. By doing so, it reveals the renewed importance of observation. But oddly enough, it is the regularly spaced conical hills representing the landscape which are totally contrived, which are not based on observation. Through this contrived landscape, we learn something about the earth and human nature.

The convention illustrated by the paintings in this chapter, the panorama, has obvious advantages. First, the broadest expanse of landscape is made possible. More important, however, this particular solution to what is essentially a spatial problem sidesteps the crucial difficulty of how to effect a successful transition from the foreground to the background. Both panoramic devices, the elevated terrace and the horizon floating behind a foreground subject, ask the spectator to suspend disbelief in order to reconcile the two quite incompatible viewpoints; at the same time, they serve to distance the spectator from the background landscape.

These devices may seem to be merely practical expedients designed to solve the problem of giving a primary subject some background. But they have powerful implications. For one, they elevate religious and noble figures to positions of authority. The view of the landscape gained by the spectator is itself authoritative, seen as if from the firmament. This is precisely the position an audience adopts when looking down at a stage from their loges; it is the amphitheatrical position. When we look at these paintings we thus feel elevated because, as spectators, we are also looking down at a panoramic landscape. Most important, these paintings surely affected the desire for actual panoramic views. It was a giant step in the history of seeing when people first appreciated idealized elevated views in pictures and then went in search of actual ones.

A Landscape Portrait

In the middle of the fifteenth century, the first "portrait" of an actual landscape was attempted. To convince the people of Geneva what the story of *The Miraculous Draught of Fishes* (fig. 6.4) might have looked like in their own day, Konrad Witz painted local fishermen and landscape features. "Thus he painted not just any lake but a lake they all knew, the lake of Geneva with the massive Mont Saleve rising in the background. It is a real landscape which everyone could see, which exists today, and still looks very much like it does in the painting."[9] Witz's contemporaries must have been excited to see their own lake as the scene of a biblical story; and the apostles as people like themselves and their neighbors.

With this technique Witz stirred the kind of emotion in his viewers which others in the fifteenth century had achieved with one-point perspective and panoramic views. When local viewers saw their own landscape pictorialized, they may have begun to look at it as though it were a painting—an object of beauty. Today just seeing a picture of the painting ignites in viewers a touristic urge not only to see the fifteenth-century painting but to go to Lake Geneva and compare it to the twentieth-century landscape.

———

Panoramic paintings, such as the few we have briefly considered in this chapter, are more naturalistic than any we have seen so far. Particular pictorial conventions produced deeper and broader views, and therefore these painted landscapes look more like the visible world. We have even seen some landscapes with "native" features that suggest that the landscapes were based not only on pictorial conventions but also on a renewed interest in depicting actual places. It should be clear, however, that to describe landscapes as naturalistic in no way implies that they are natural, or independent of culture. On the contrary, they are views of agricultural countrysides and towns, contrived images of scientific principles and biblical stories. They are in all cases images of modified lands, which are not natural in the sense in which the eighteenth-century English made the world understand the term.

Fig. 6.4. Konrad Witz, *The Miraculous Draught of Fishes* (1444). Genf Museum, Geneva. (Foto Marburg/ Art Resource, New York.)

Even further, the point of view assumed in these panoramas is entirely cultural. In all of them, landscape is secondary and is not highlighted. Instead, these paintings elevated religious and noble figures, and the patrons who viewed them. Such elevation remains a standard pictorial convention, indeed a standard scenic habit, even today.

Presenting a panoramic propsect not only empowered the spectator but also accelerated the desire for paintings in which landscape is the primary subject. It is precisely to such paintings that we shall next turn.

7

Bewildering the Spectator: The Northern Renaissance

Sixteenth-century artists and their patrons lived in an urban civilization that had learned how to exert some control over natural forces. Consequently, they could look at the landscape with a certain detachment not felt before. Storms, forests, floods, mountains, and fire became subjects both distant and exciting. The security that artists felt in their urban environment, combined with their determination to explore new avenues of landscape depiction, led them to paint landscapes that were both pleasurable and horrifying. These paintings were intended to incite emotion rather than relate information, and they were infused with the idea of wilderness, of that which is bewildering and uncontrollable. This pictorialization of terrifying natural forces in order to generate excitement is clear evidence of an increasing confidence in the ability to control such forces.

Following the development of perspective and the panorama in central Italy, progress in landscape painting during the sixteenth century moved northward, first to the area around Venice. In fact, it was in Venice that the term *landscape (paese)* was first applied to an individual painting.[1] "The Venetian State was very closely involved in land drainage and reclamation, and many of those directly engaged in the processes of land transformation were equally involved in the artistic representation of landscape."[2] Such a coincidence of interest is often to be found. In other words, it is common that interest in landscape painting occurs in urban cultures at precisely the time when the land is undergoing drastic changes in use or ownership. This is precisely the situation we shall observe in nineteenth-century America.

Northern Europeans carried over their interest in the land and in natural forces to painting. Also at the beginning of the sixteenth century, the pastoral ideal was reinvigorated by Renaissance poets.[3] In the paintings we shall look at now, the landscape is slowly, but aggressively, overcoming the foreground subjects to which it had been subordinate in earlier centuries.

The First Pictured Pastoral

In Virgil's first eclogue, Meliboeus was exiled from his harmonious pastoral setting and plunged into the chaos of nature and an unpredictable society beyond the pasture. Even though Tityrus remained safely ensconced within the pastoral ideal, Virgil made it clear that he was naive about the world outside. It is precisely this combination of elements—the pictorialization of life's uncertainty as well as the visual expression of the pastoral ideal—that is depicted for the first time by Giorgione.

The *Tempest* (fig. 7.1) is a painting whose subject has confounded scholars since the Renaissance.[4] Recently, Edgar Wind has supplied convincing arguments that Giorgione's painting is a pastoral allegory in which Constancy, represented by a man, and Love, represented by a woman nursing her child, are dramatically placed in a setting of Chance, represented by a turbulent storm that we see roiling the sky. "Undaunted by the threats of the rising tempest, emblematic of capricious Fortune, they display the martial confidence and the maternal affection that befit 'a soldier and a gypsy'—characters whose unsettled mode of life has made them familiars of *Fortuna*. Uncertainty is their natural element, the congenial setting for their virtues. Hence the mysterious unison between the landscape and figures, which has always been felt to be the essence of the painting."[5]

If Wind's theory is accurate, then Giorgione has not fallen prey to a sentimental view of a domesticated nature. In other words, these figures do not represent Tityrus's naive view, the view of a man protected from the world outside the pasture. Instead, Giorgione has pictured precisely what Meliboeus had to face outside the pasture: chance, both in nature's forces and the vagaries of the city. Although the spectator may be alarmed by the tumultuous sky threatening to destroy the pastoral calm, the figures are not. The woman who looks assuredly into the eyes of the spectator is certainly aware of, but untroubled by, the tempest.

In the *Tempest,* natural forces are the dominant theme from which the significance of the figures is derived. In pictorializing natural forces in this secular landscape, however, Giorgione has given form to the pastoral ideal. It is the precise combination of features with which we have become so utterly familiar: a stream running through a grove of trees opens the central space to the sky. A bridge crossing the stream separates the town from its rural setting and contributes to the intimacy of refuge provided the figures, whose ease reinforces the theme of pastoral inaction.

Giorgione's pastoral is particularly important to our study because it is representative of the pictorial model upon which is based the structure of the English landscape garden, whose development is *the* critical chapter in the history of seeing the landscape, as well as in

Fig. 7.1. Giorgione, *The Tempest* (1505–10). Accademia, Venice. (Alinari/Art Resource, New York.)

the history of our own parks. Even in Giorgione's sixteenth-century version of the Virgilian landscape, we can already see hints of Central Park. In the free space of the center we can, for example, imagine a long meadow surrounded by dark masses of trees.

The influence of Giorgione, who was himself influenced by the pictorial conventions inherited from the stage, came to the English landscape garden through the work of another artist, Claude Lorrain, the painter most preferred by the eighteenth-century English. Commenting on Giorgione, Clark makes this connection clear: "On either side are dark masses of tree and rock, like wings of a theatrical scene, which leave the center of the picture free. Even the figures, which are completely one with the landscape, are sometimes placed at the side; sky and distance take the principal place. It is the composition which, with every refinement of variation, was to form the basis of Claude."[6]

Not only did the English hang Claude's paintings on their walls but they depended upon the compositional conventions he had inherited from Giorgione when they redesigned the landscape outside their homes.

Although Claude refined Giorgione's pastoral depiction, he omitted the ominous character of the storm-swept landscape. This was not the case with Salvator Rosa, a contemporary of Claude, nor with the several other painters to whom we shall turn next. In their works we shall see how the wilderness was framed and thereby "de-natured." Indeed, we shall see that paintings by Altdorfer and Bosch package wilderness and make it accessible in a manner that is in an important sense similar to our own experience of visiting a national park.

Wilderness

The adjective *wild* has long conveyed the idea of being lost or confused. An early version of *wilderness* was conceived when the Old English *deor* (animal) was prefixed with *wild* to denote an uncontrollable creature. One of the earliest uses of the word is in the eighth-century epic *Beowulf*, in which *wildeor* appeared in reference to savage and fantastic beasts inhabiting a dismal region of forests, crags, and cliffs.[7] The association of *wilderness* with forests is understandable because the term's roots are found in the languages of heavily forested northern Europe.

Paolo Pino, an Italian writing in the middle of the sixteenth century, tried to account for the particular development of landscape by painters of northern Europe. "The Northerners show a special gift for painting landscapes because they portray the scenery of their own homeland, which offers most suitable motifs by virtue of its wildness, while we Italians live in the garden of the world, which is more delightful to behold in reality than in a painting."[8]

The idea that northerners were more gifted landscape painters because they depicted native features, as Pino has argued, does not exactly fit with the images. It is precisely "scenery"—stage properties—rather than native features which we will see depicted in the northerners' paintings. Sixteenth-century northern painters used a minimum of firsthand observation and the complete repertoire of compositional conventions inherited from the theater and Italian painting to create their fantastic and novel landscapes. Instead of being views of actual places, these paintings are largely accumulations of individual features, very few of which are derived from the artists' native lands.

Pino argued that it was the "wildness" of the north that further contributed to the success of the northern landscape in pictures. Although he was one of the first to manifest an interest in "wildness," once again we must remember that his interest was not an expression of a desire to be lost or confused. It was instead an interest in the concept, the cultural construction, of "wildness." The word *wildness,* like the word *nature,* lacks a concrete referent—that is, there is no specific object that we can call "wildness." The term designates a quality that produces a certain mood or feeling. What Paolo Pino really means is this: wildness is better for pictures.

Pino's idea that wildness is more delightful in paintings than in real life might seem quite contrary to our own perceptions. After all, we think of a trip to the wildness in our national parks as a valuable experience. But it is vital to remember that our parks are carefully framed enclaves. We take vacations just to face challenges different from those of our daily lives. Getting lost, feeling our thighs throbbing from uphill climbs, and seeing the sudden movement of an unknown creature may arouse feelings of fear, but they are followed quickly by comforting reminders: a hot shower and a good dinner await wilderness spectators in the Yellowstone Hotel. In the sixteenth century, largely uninhabited lands produced feelings of terror; but framed within painted canvases they were, like our own wilderness hikes, pleasurable and exciting.

Albrecht Altdorfer expressed this mixed attitude toward the wilderness better than anyone before him. "[Altdorfer] is the most German of all painters, for although his eye penetrates deeply into the northern forest with its twisting tendrils and undergrowth, its pools and mosses glowing like enamel, he views them with a certain *gemuetlichkeit,* a smugness, as though from the inside of a cottage window."[9] To paint wilderness makes the contrast between the spectator and subject more explicit, the contrast between chaos and order more dramatic. It heightens the effect of security and power which the painting bestows on the spectator.

In Altdorfer's painting *Landscape with Satyr Family* (fig. 7.2), we see a broadleaf forest, teeming with growth, that has pressed itself into the foreground so that as spectators we have some sense of bewilderment. The figures—part beast, part human—are clearly not having a picnic. Huddled together, they fear even their immediate surroundings. Even a detached spectator can sense their apprehension. That same spectator can also easily be transported by the conventions of framing through a carefully composed vista, formed by coulisses, to the larger, and distanced, landscape.

Fig. 7.2. Albrecht Altdorfer, *Landscape with Satyr Family* (1507). Staatliche Museen Preussischer Kulturbesitz, Gemaeldegalerie, Berlin.

Painterly Fire

One of the strangest and most imaginative landscapes ever painted was *Garden of Earthly Delights,* created by Hieronymus Bosch at the beginning of the sixteenth century. It is an altarpiece of three sections: *Garden of Eden* is the left panel, *Garden of Earthly Delights* is the central piece, and *Hell* (fig. 7.3) is the right panel. In the earthly garden sensuality prevails, but in hell man is tormented as his landscape burns.

Bosch may have been inspired to paint flames by medieval miniatures or by the frequent representation of hell in stage plays.[10] The visual excitement of unexpected red and orange in a pool of darkness added to his popularity; in the next thirty years Bosch's flames break out in almost every landscape.

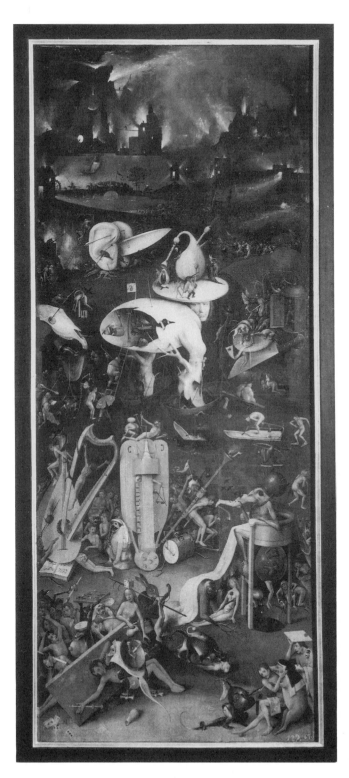

Fig. 7.3. Hieronymus Bosch, *Hell*, right-hand panel of *Garden of Earthly Delights* (c. 1505). Museo del Prado, Madrid.

'Three-quarters of a century after Bosch's picture was painted, the first detailed treatise on landscape painting was written.[11] Its author was a painter by the name of Cristoforo Sorte, who had been exposed to paintings of Flemish night scenes of burning cities which had probably been influenced by the hell landscapes by Bosch. One of the experiences Sorte describes in his treatise illustrates how pictorializations of powerful natural forces can lead to treating an actual experience as if it were a picture.

One night Sorte was aroused by a raging fire. Instead of experiencing horror and fear, he stopped for a while to admire the "'marvellous effects of that fire because the places nearby and far away were at the same time illuminated by three different splendors.'" Later, in his treatise, he described "in truly painterly terms the red glow of the flames, the reflection of the scene in the tremulous waters of the Adige and the effect of the moonlight on the billows of smoke which merged with the clouds. 'And as I was a painter at that time,'" he concluded, "'I imitated it all in colours.'"[12] Sorte's acquaintance with Flemish paintings of burning cities had taught him to experience an actual fire pictorially. The inescapable fact is that the aesthetic beauty of the fire detached him from the horror he was seeing. This is truly an example of the pictorialization of nature and the development of a basic scenic habit. For example, consider our own acquaintance with pictorial violence. After having seen an endless stream of carefully composed deaths and wounds in motion pictures, or the beauty of the atomic bomb we have seen replayed time and again on television, aren't we encouraged to detach ourselves from actual violence and to see it instead as a picture?

Landscape Collage

One follower of Bosch, according to Kenneth Clark, was Pieter Brueghel, the greatest Dutch artist of his day. Brueghel placed flames in a field of snow to create contrasts of color and temperature. He also inaugurated a new type of landscape—the forest interior. This technique provided further framing to effectively engage the spectator in a picture of a forest. In *Hunters in the Snow* (fig. 7.4), Brueghel has combined the forest interior with a distant landscape panorama like that which we saw in Italian paintings.

The spectator's view is elevated just above the peasants in the foreground standing with their dogs and tending a fire. They are on a ledge overlooking an enormous panorama. Beyond the trees we can see all the necessary components of village life, and in the distance, the steepest of mountains. It is through formidable compositional techniques that the artist succeeded in giving the spectator such a range of topographic experience. Regional landscape features that

Fig. 7.4. Pieter Brueghel, *Hunters in the Snow* (1565). Kunsthistoriches Museum, Vienna. (Foto Marburg/ Art Resource, New York.)

are geographically incompatible have been expertly glued together: threatening Alpine ranges contrast with the innocent domesticity of a Flemish village, the two joined by a torrential river that belongs, in reality, to neither landscape.

Even though Brueghel draws remote pieces of landscape together, he is considered "the one master of naturalistic landscape between Bellini and the seventeenth century."[13] By now we understand that "naturalistic" in no way means "natural" in the sense that the landscape pictured is untouched, or even an actual place. Instead, it means that Brueghel has created a convincingly realistic view. What we see in this painting is not only a collage of landscapes but also a collage of attitudes toward the landscape. The northern manner of walking right into the terrors of "nature," in pictures, at least, has been abruptly joined to the lofty Renaissance view of "nature" we have seen above.

Recognizable Expression

With El Greco's *View of Toledo* (fig. 7.5) we come to a picture that is extremely expressionistic, even troubling. The landscape is tortured

Fig. 7.5. El Greco, *View of Toledo* (1604–14). Bequest of Mrs. H. O. Havemyer, 1929; The H. O. Havemyer Collection, 1929 (29.100.6), Metropolitan Museum of Art, New York.

and tense. It is warped and slipping down the canvas. The spectator senses that some kind of transfiguring power has heaped the hills of a gorge into juxtaposed masses; foreground vegetation takes the form of flames. The buildings strung along the ridges are spectral and sinister; the ragged storm cloud surging behind them swells and streams away as if to wrap the whole of Spain in a smoky pall. Rich forest greens in the foreground are emphasized by distant deep rich blues from the ominous sky reflecting back on the buildings. Once again, the conventions of picturing have simultaneously enhanced the sinister power that rages across this landscape, and have made the viewer feel secure.

Like some of the early panoramic landscapes, however, this expressionistic landscape is a recognizable place. Amid this force and frenzy, the city of Toledo and its surroundings remain identifiable.

No other artist of the time, not even El Greco himself, who produced other remarkable views of the city he had made his home, ever again gave this quality of fantasy to an actual place.

———

Aristotle wrote that "human beings naturally love imitation. Even when the thing being imitated is horrible and people wouldn't like looking at the original, they still like seeing the image of that which is horrible, like a corpse or a monster."[14] The painters we have briefly surveyed in this chapter have depicted natural forces in order to deliberately excite a pleasing sensation of horror. The paintings we have seen in this chapter are the first ever to glorify uncontrollable forces within a subject matter that is primarily landscape. As we shall see, pictorialization is a means of safely expressing, and thereby controlling, fear. In landscape architectural practice, where the need to control forms and materials as well as to provide a safe environment is obvious, the glorification of uncontrollable forces frequently, however, yields to pictorialization, whereby changing processes are subdued, diversity is reduced, or a comfortable image of nature, such as the pastoral ideal, is substituted.

8

Landscape Prospects: The Seventeenth Century

The seventeenth century brought profound changes in the scenic habits of the Western world. Retinal images were described as pictures, the first box camera with a lens for viewing landscapes was constructed,[1] and not incidentally, landscape became, for the first time ever, the primary subject of many paintings. The pictures we shall look at in this chapter were painted in Italy and Holland but—and for our purpose this is their most important contribution—they made an unforgettable impression on eighteenth-century English eyes, becoming, as we shall see, models for the landscape garden.

Italian Landscape

In order to absorb some of the culture of the ancient world and the Renaissance, eighteenth-century English connoisseurs went to Italy. In Rome they saw landscape paintings. Their descriptions of their travels across the Alps and through Italy "are unmistakable evidence that they were influenced to find beauty in a particular sort of landscape—elaborate, wide-spread, greatly diversified, and having classical association—the landscape, that is, of the seventeenth-century Roman landscape painters."[2]

During the seventeenth century, Claude Lorrain and Salvator Rosa had already created an audience anxious to see the landscape in painting. They were the first painters to do so. "Not until about 1640 was landscape fully established in the lay mind as a separate and important branch of painting. By that year both Claude and Rosa were well on their way to being the fashion, and the fashion they remained for a hundred and fifty years. From 1640 on, they could not satisfy the commissions which poured in upon them from prelates, princes, and nobles, and until they died their pictures were sought for, extravagantly valued, copied, imitated, forged."[3] As we shall see, not only were the works of Claude and Rosa imitated in oil paint and ink, but in England they would be transformed into actual three-dimensional landscapes. Indeed, these are the two painters who most successfully depicted landscapes that aroused passions in eighteenth-century English spectators.

The pastoral tradition in painting, which began with the Roman Odyssey Landscapes (fig. 3.4) and was reinvigorated by Giorgione in *The Tempest* fifteen centuries later (fig. 7.1), was perfected in the seventeenth century by Claude Lorrain, known simply as Claude. Together these paintings have so formed our scenic habits that we have learned to look for wooded scenes that have a central open space, dark green foregrounds, light green middle grounds, and blue distances. When we recognize this composition in an actual place (e.g., Prospect Park in Brooklyn, New York), we can exclaim with all the authority bequeathed to us by centuries of acculturation, "This is a beautiful landscape!"

In the hands of Claude, the Arcadian landscape was so thoroughly and consistently developed as a pictorial theme that it has remained with us through painted images even if we have not read Virgil. Claude's paintings are pictures of perfect harmony. Tityrus would feel at home in Claude's landscapes, and so do spectators who view them. The idea of escaping from both society and nature to a comfortable and secure setting seems to be enduringly attractive. Claude's paintings represent just such an ideal place, a mental refuge from the real world.

Even though Claude's work is in no sense "natural" but instead presents an illusion realistically, it also represents a peak in the development of naturalistic landscape painting. His figures are at ease in, though overwhelmed by, an agriculturally maintained landscape. Landscape has finally become the primary subject, and Claude's depictions of it are most convincing even though they do not reproduce actual views.

Claude's work did, however, involve observing actual places. He lived in Rome but visited the countryside to draw and observe light patterns. There he noted the massing of trees and the effects of shadows on the landscape. It would, however, have been quite foreign to Claude's conception of his art to have painted a picture directly from observation, for he sharply distinguished his studies from his paintings. His studies were sketches made on the basis of observation, and he did not consider them ends in themselves. Instead, he would, with great artifice, select, sort, rearrange, and unify disparate elements from them in order to produce compositions that gave the appearance of "natural" carelessness. In other words, he would subordinate all his powers of observation and knowledge of appearances to the production of a unified composition.

Claude's compositions depended on conventions that had been introduced by earlier paintings: woods opened by pastures, coulisse for achieving atmospheric distances, topographic relief, and the presence of water. Using these conventions, however, he composed an ideal view, arranging elements to achieve an image of harmony, that is, the pastoral ideal. With Claude, each of the conventions was strengthened to perfect an illusion whose primary theme was space and distance.

Claude perfected the use of coulisse. By using forms that edge into the foreground to frame the canvas, he also created the appearance of greater depth in a scene. In *A Pastoral* (fig. 8.1), he has pruned a vista from the trees and rendered a dark and deemphasized foreground; it frames no specific subject but space itself. This vast extent of space emphasizes landscape by reducing people, palace, sheep, and cattle to insignificance.

The outcome of the conventions is to elevate the patron-viewer into the amphitheatrical viewing position we recall from the design of early theaters. Spectators look down upon shepherds who rest just inside the picture plane; they are directing us to look across the distance toward the far country villa. "The initial movement in all Claude's landscape is this one, from the foreground straight to the far distance; and it must I think be understood as a rapid movement, an immediate response to the way the picture is organized."[4]

Fig. 8.1. Claude Lorrain, *A Pastoral* (1648). Leo C. Hanna, Jr., Fund, Yale University Art Gallery, New Haven, Connecticut.

The landscape in a painting by Claude has been arranged to raise the spectator's eyes to the horizon. One of the chief ways this is done is with a series of horizontal bands. Each one identifies a topographic change across which the spectator's eye leaps in order to reach the distance. In the foreground of *A Pastoral,* for example, we see a dark band representing a small ridge lightly shaded on its crest. Against the ridge is another, darker band representing an embankment. The river itself reads as a lighter band whose surface is reflecting sunlight and whose bank on the other side is formed by yet another dark band. Beyond the river three more bands, suffused with a clear yellow evening light, lead back to the distant villa. Beyond the villa two more form a body of water, and an island. Several more bands form mountains, and finally the eye is taken by the last blue band to the sky.

Claude had created a new device for contributing to the illusion of distance: "It is clear, in the first place, that however instinctive and habitual it became to see a view in terms of a series of horizontal bands, nevertheless to think of perspective in terms of a series of abrupt leaps into the distance, and not as a gradual diminution in the size of things, did represent definite modifications of perspective which had been developed in the Renaissance."[5]

In practice, this was a change that meant that a certain composition of the landscape became obligatory. There had to be both topographic bands and objects to smooth the transitions between them. The spectator's viewpoint had to be on rising ground. The trees and buildings had to be disposed in such a way that the shadows they made would differentiate a particular band from those above and below it.[6] The effect totally charmed the English gentry. "There was something in Claude's gentle poetry, in his wistful glances at a vanished civilization and in a feeling that all nature could be laid out for man's delight, *like a gentleman's park,* which appealed particularly to the English connoisseurs of the eighteenth century."[7]

The setting in one of Claude's paintings may be a seaport, a wooded dell, or a watered plain. Regardless, there generally are screens of dark trees to the left or the right, or sometimes even at the center, which form stagelike wings that intensify the central light. Occasionally, a classical temple appears in the cool shadows and some insignificant figure addresses a familiar subject inconspicuously in the foreground. It should be apparent, therefore, that in Claude's landscapes the attempt is not to accurately portray an actual place but to create the illusion of a harmonious pastoral landscape.

The singular, and indeed the overwhelming, contribution of eighteenth-century England to the formation of our scenic habits is the result of the landscape itself having been changed to imitate Claude's paintings. It should be clear that to achieve Claude's painterly effects in an actual place, to apply his compositional principles in order to create an actual view, the landscape would have to be totally recomposed. And it was, in the eighteenth-century landscape garden.

To recreate Claude's "topographic" bands in the landscape and increase the perception of depth, rolling topography had to be constructed to lead the spectator's eyes into the distance. Rivers, bridges, distant structures, and grazing animals further distinguished one topographic band from another. Clumps of trees, acting like coulisses, were used to frame views and increase depth. The creation of deep vistas, irregularly balanced, provided the same theme in the garden that it had in Claude's paintings: refuge.[8]

The idea of refuge which Claude depicted for his patrons was easily adopted by the land-owning gentry in eighteenth-century England (and by American city dwellers in nineteenth-century parks, and executives in twentieth-century corporate headquarters). After all, Claude's view of landscape was entirely anthropocentric. His trees created pleasant shade for an outing; his peasants gave spectators the illusion of pastoral paradise, not of toiling for a living. Picturesque ruins and well-washed peasants were recognizable as being associated with noble Romans, an association the English, who saw themselves as inheritors of classical civilization, were eager to accept.

Claude is the most ardent worshipper of the *genius loci,* "the spirit of the place," yet another theme that the English would use to invest their landscape with classical notions.[9] Claude's use of the *genius loci* has been described as giving the spectator the feeling that "some god is in this place." "Never, it is true, one of the greater gods: no mysterious and fearful Pan, no soul-stirring Bacchus or all-embracing Demeter; scarcely, though he tried more than once deliberately to invoke them, Apollo and the Muses, but some mild local deity, the inhabitant of a rustic shrine whose presence only heightens the glamour of the scene."[10] By acquiring Claude's rustic deity, the English were able to *re-place* in England's rural landscape classical ideas from the ancient world.

Claude has made generations of painters feel that the Roman *campagna* (countryside) provided the only scenery worthy of a serious landscape painter. Even if they could not afford a journey to Rome, Claude's followers still transformed their native countryside into a reflection of the Roman countryside.[11] The English so successfully reflected Claude's images in their own landscape that when we recreate them today—even in Texas—we categorize them, somewhat mistakenly, as landscapes native to England.

Recalling Virgil's classical pastoral, the *Eclogues,* we are reminded that the idea of the pasture was more complex than a simple paradise. But where is Meliboeus in Claude's vision? Where is Giorgione's powerful tempest, which represented the uncertainty and potential violence of nature? The only sense of uncertainty in Claude's landscapes—the sense that something might break up, or intrude upon,

Claude's rural harmony—results from the fact that the images are
touched with a certain wistfulness, as if Claude knew that this per-
fection could last no longer than the moment in which it takes possession of the mind.[12] In the painting to follow, we shall see a landscape that does not appear to treat its inhabitants with such utter
benevolence.

SALVATOR ROSA

The myth of the pastoral ideal rendered by Claude, the myth in
which Tityrus lived on the fruits of the earth, peacefully, piously, and
simply, is exactly opposite to the conception of human history that
produced, for example, Altdorfer's *Landscape with Satyr Family* (fig.
7.2) and the painting we shall look at now. Salvator Rosa excites
spectators with ideas of a primitive past. This very different conception was depicted by quite different forms. In contrast to the smooth
volumes and regular placement that we have seen in Claude, broken
surfaces, jagged contours, and harsh textures characterize Rosa.

In the eighteenth century, Rosa's name was used as a label to describe actual English landscapes: wild and rugged, usually mountainous places, with expressive trees, and gloomy and often stormy
skies. Many English tourists had been introduced to Rosa's work on
their trips to Italy, and invoked his name on their return passage over
the Alps, as well as in letters describing the journey. Many of them
believed that Rosa had painted the very Alpine scenery they were
awed by, even though he had not.[13] Like Claude's paintings, Rosa's
are of no actual place, although their naturalism is equally as effective in convincing the spectator of their authenticity.

The landscapes that most appealed to Rosa were rocky and forested, relatively untrodden and abrupt, and he enhanced them with
strange, theatrical rock formations, mountains honeycombed with
fearful caves, trees writhing on the cliff tops, and other startling or
fantastic features. In *Landscape with Travelers Asking the Way* (fig.
8.2), we see tree branches criss-crossed and spiky, blasted by generations of thunderbolts. Barren rocks and ragged trees form coulisses to
give the spectator a deep view into space.

The travelers who are asking for direction are subordinate to, and
overpowered by, the landscape. We can think of them as the forerun-
ners of eighteenth-century travelers who would be inspired by Rosa
to return to England to look for sublime scenes. Such travelers, because they were motivated by pictures, were ancestors of twentieth-
century tourists. Though they deserve to be called travelers rather
than tourists because of the difficulty of their journeys, Rosa's paintings inspired them to go in search of scenes filled with terror and
foreboding.

Rosa's landscapes were popularly believed to have been peopled with *banditti.* "These bandits were, it seems, at least to some, human beings freed from the fetters of society and also in a rather unspecific way at war with governments and established values."[14] What the *banditti* stood for, Rosa also represented to eighteenth-century English connoisseurs: an artist who was an outlaw, outside of artistic convention. Painting wild images of the landscape, he could be understood as an artist whose inspiration came from his heart and from the contemplation of nature rather than from academic training or society.

Since his admirers had such a romantic understanding of Rosa's inspiration, they became very interested in his personal life. Rosa "was seen as a wild, romantic, independent figure, a self-styled outlaw, grimly and stoically laughing at the follies and disappointments of the world, anti-academic, remaining true to the dictates of his own heart and mind, unsullied by any compromise with patrons, conventions or traditions, except those which he himself freely accepted."[15] We recall that Giotto had been the first artist to sign his name to his work. Here we can observe another increase in the amount of attention paid to the individual artist: his personal life begins to be observed.

Rosa's paintings also were taken to be particularly imaginative. Consider the following statement from Manwaring's *Italian Landscape in Eighteenth-Century England:*

Fig. 8.2. Salvator Rosa, *Landscape with Travelers Asking the Way* (1640s). Collection of Sir Denis Mahon, London.

I once did see a landscape of Salvator's which taught me what an imaginative thing a landscape may be. . . . Such shaggy rocks,— such dark and ruinous caves,—such spectre-eyed, serpent-headed trees, wreathed and contorted into hideous mimicry of human shape, as if by the struggles of human spirits incarcerated in their trunks,—such horrid depths of shade,—such fearful visitations of strange light,—such horrid likenesses.[16]

Was Rosa then a seventeenth-century Meliboeus who intended to destabilize conventions? Meliboeus confronted a destructive, harsh, unjust nature and was filled with fear. Similarly, Rosa depicted the destructive forces of nature. On the other hand, he clearly gave trees human shapes. Was he telling us that we are one with nature? Perhaps. This, if course, would be quite contrary to Meliboeus, who found that nature was oblivious to humans. Rosa shows us that even the wildest and most rugged landscapes are easily grasped. His scenes can be traversed and appreciated visually. His images thus leave the viewer with a sentimental attitude toward wilderness, not a true "Meliboean" one. Even though Rosa's wilderness is wildly beautiful, it is finally within our control.

Rosa's pictures do indeed follow the naturalistic conventions for depicting landscape which we have been examining. Even the wildest of scenes offers a sense of prospect and refuge to both the figures and the spectator. The spectator is afforded a feeling of security, comfort, and control. "There was a schematic quality in both Picturesque landscape and the Salvatorial 'sublime' which tended to reduce art to a formula, and an easily learnt one at that. It was, ultimately, too easy to invoke the name of Salvator Rosa in relation to rugged and wild landscapes."[17] Nevertheless, Rosa's landscapes opened up a new vein of sentiment for wildness—a sentiment that today could not be generated by the same pictorial formula. For in most of the United States even actual "wildernesses" today are maintained to such an extent that it is difficult to even imagine terror.

Dutch Landscape

Late in the sixteenth century, the word *landscape* entered the English language, imported from Holland along with Dutch paintings of scenery, or *landschap*.[18] In English, *landscape* was first used to describe a representation of a countryside, either as the background or the subject of a picture. Later the word came to mean a piece of the actual countryside which lay in prospect: that is, an extensive piece of the landscape which could be seen from a fixed point of view, as in a painting.[19] It is not surprising that the word we have inherited from painting to describe the land we see is of Dutch origin, for Dutch painters were richly observant of their native landscape.

Why would Dutch painters depict the landscape more observantly than any before them? One explanation argues for the influence of the theory of vision that was devised at the beginning of the seventeenth century. Johannes Kepler, for example, described retinal images as "pictures." Not only did he use the word *picture* but he also described the colored rays of visible light as "painted" on the retina. Even the word he chose for that which did the painting is a word that translates as "little brushes."[20] Naturalistic painting had achieved such convincing illusions of the world that it supplied the metaphors used to explain eyesight itself.

The influence of these metaphors on seventeenth-century attitudes toward both seeing and painting was extensive. Vision was thought of as a mechanical process whereby a "representation" of the world is reproduced on the retina. The observer's experience was detached from seeing. The making of pictures, with this metaphor in mind, was considered to be not a selection process or a matter of judgment but a matter of mirroring. Dutch artists, then, perceived their role as capturing or receiving what is seen, and re-presenting it just as the eye does.[21]

A painting such as *Market by the Seashore* (fig. 8.3) is a representation of the world, seemingly unconcerned with the spectator's presence. It is trying neither to picture an ideal nor to evoke terror. In *The Art of Describing*, Svetlana Alpers argues that Dutch art contrasts with the art of the Italian Renaissance because it does not include significant human actions; instead, it describes "the world seen." As a result, several of the pictorial conventions employed by the Dutch contrast with those we have already observed. They are interesting, however, precisely because of this contrast. Even if Alpers is correct, and the ultimate purpose of Dutch art is to describe what is seen, it nevertheless remains the case that paintings by someone such as van Ruysdael are not natural—that is, devoid of culturally influenced perception—in the slightest.

One Dutch convention that contrasts with Italian Renaissance conventions is the frequent absence of a positioned viewer. Unlike the spectator of early perspective painting, whose attention was centered on a single vanishing point, the viewer of Dutch painting is "neither located nor characterized, perceiving all with an attentive eye but leaving no trace."[22] The consequence of this deemphasis is an image that seems as though it had existed prior to the spectator.

Another contrasting convention is permeable framing. In it, the image appears to be less carefully selected, less forcefully composed and balanced than a Renaissance painting. By contrast, Alpers likens a Dutch landscape painting to a mirror or a map, or one of the many

Fig. 8.3. Salomon van Ruysdael, *Market by the Seashore* (1629). Bequest of Rupert L. Joseph, 1959 (60.55.4), Metropolitan Museum of Art, New York.

frames of a movie, an unbounded fragment of a world that the camera might have continued to pan. Above all, the view is not to be grasped or entered into as one-point perspective invites the spectator to do. It is just there for the looking.

One might assume, then, that if Alpers believes that Dutch painters were more observant of the world, she would say that their paintings are more natural. However, she does not. "These features are commonly explained by an appeal to nature. The Dutch artist, the argument goes, adds actual viewing experience to the artificial perspective system of the Italians. An imitative picture, it is assumed, is perspectival and Italian by definition and the Dutch add nature to it. . . . But the appeal to nature leaves us justifiably uncomfortable. Nature cannot solve the question of art."[23]

In painting as in design, to describe a composition as natural is to deny its cultural roots. The harmonious landscape pictured in Claude's paintings and then transferred to the English landscape garden, the wildness depicted by Salvator Rosa and sought by generations of travelers and tourists, and the natural-seeming Dutch paintings are all specific art forms and are anything but natural. Understanding this fact about them helps us to understand our own scenic habits and to realize that the landscape, whether it is pictured or designed, is a product of cultural forces.

Although the word *landscape* may have entered the English language to describe a prospect, as in a painting and later an actual view, a closer look at the Dutch origins of the word reveals quite a different meaning. "'Landscape' as a word seems to originate in Frisian [a Germanic language of the Dutch province of Friesland] to describe the made land recovered from the North Sea. That is, from the very beginning the word has been almost violently Cultural in its implications."[24]

Indeed, "landscape," modified land, is one of the most characteristic features of the Netherlands. Unlike the forests of northern Europe or the hilly, cultivated landscape of Italy, the Netherlands is an exposed, flooding landscape, and the open space afforded by water is endemic to the culture. If, as described earlier, the Dutch artist is determined to represent what the eye sees, then the native landscape is going to be a primary subject of pictures.

In *Market by the Seashore* (fig. 8.3), by Salomon van Ruysdael, we see an eye-level view that, in sharp distinction to that of Claude, does not locate the spectator in the condition of prospect and refuge. Even though we might be familiar with modern painting, the sight of a picture of a prospect without the corresponding refuge for the spectator is quite surprising. Compare, for example, Salomon van Ruysdael's dunescape to the dizzy Renaissance prospect Brueghel attached to a Flemish village in figure 7.4. The dunescape is a dramatic coming down to earth. "The horizon and point of view have descended toward the surface, and if there is a raised prospect, it is on the scale of an authentically Netherlandish dune or hummock, not a spuriously Flemish Alp. Grandeur has been replaced by intimacy, universality by locality, a Platonic vision of a unified creation by an Aristotelian one of randomly scattered things. It is a world that has been deprogrammed. Figures and their elements no longer march about their business or issue in angry eruptions: they labor, they idle, they trudge."[25]

As spectators, we are not comforted by the refuge of coulisse or the sure stationing of linear perspective. We are not even elevated onlookers; the peasants stand above us on a dune. To spectators who have become familiar with the conventions we have been following, features of this painting, such as an absence of reassuring reference points, can be disturbing. Boundaries that we expect will provide definition are broken or blown away. There is no scenery. These figures are not decoratively strolling about like noblemen surveying their property or shepherds leading the good life. The native habitat is not prettied up; the violently eroded shoreline has met a powerful force.

In a crucial sense, however, this painting is no more realistic or objective than one by Claude. Even though it reveals an acute obser-

vation of life and landscape, it was created, like other seventeenth-
century paintings, in a studio. As a result, it is a highly selective and
value-laden presentation of a particular native habitat, and thus represents the substitution of one kind of subjectivity for another (e.g.,
that exhibited by Claude). This "native habitat" is not simply one
of terrain, vegetation, and climate; it is formed by a community at
a specific time and in a specific landscape. It is a communal frontier
freshly presented.

The painters of Protestant Holland faced a market-based economy
and a democracy. Instead of receiving commissions, they had to paint
their pictures first and then find buyers. The buyers—the public—
proved an even more tyrannical master than the single patron. Again,
as before, it seems a safe conjecture that most of the buyers of early
native landscapes were urban.[26] The Dutch who bought many hundreds of these paintings must have been moved by something like pa-
triotic images: representations of their own landscape and industries.

PETER PAUL RUBENS

After the 1630s, according to Simon Schama, Dutch landscape was
once again revised, this time from the homespun and local to the pol-
ished and cosmopolitan. A more cultivated generation of patrons
found coarse representations of peasants unpleasing. The fisherfolk
were replaced by figures drawn more from pastoral lyric poetry than
from seashore and duneland doggerel.[27] The trees were manicured,

Fig. 8.4. Peter Paul Rubens, *Autumn Landscape with Castle Steen* (after 1635). National Gallery, London.

the water still, the air sweet. We return to boundaries emphatically stated to define ownership. *Autumn Landscape with Castle Steen* (fig. 8.4), by Peter Paul Rubens, is a hybrid of native and conventional themes, and, significantly for this study, it is the type of landscape favored by English connoisseurs.

The painter of this image, the viewer of the actual place, and the owner of the estate are one—Rubens himself. It is Rubens's possession of such a bucolic retreat that gives this prospect its authority. It looks outward to a deep and distant, even a flat, landscape. Trees define a refuge around the castle and expose the distance. In sum, the painting elevates the spectator in more ways than one.

The prospect of Flanders stretching out to the right is the view seen from Rubens's house. It is suitably graced by a golden light. Such views of cities mark not only the fact that in seventeenth-century Holland one was seldom far from an urban center but also the fact that cities were seen as part of the land. This reveals that the contrast, even the tension, between city and country which is such a traditional feature of Western urban culture was not decisive in Holland.

This painting records Rubens's cherished dream of becoming a member of the landed gentry. Consequently, it is dominated by the proprietorial presence of Castle Steen. Many of the landscape paintings from the 1660s are at the service of a social process that transformed commercial oligarchs into landed gentry. Not surprisingly, many of these paintings were highly esteemed by and bought by the eighteenth-century English elite who were engaged in the same process.

Although just behind the picture plane we can see a hunter aiming for a bird and a wagon carrying a trussed lamb on the way to market, this is not a working countryside. The laborers are scenically placed. What Rubens creates here is the landscape as park. And in this composition, which combines native features of the countryside with traditional conventions for depicting a prospect, he lays out the representational plan that the English would perfect in the landscape garden.[28] In their choice of motifs, paintings such as those of Rubens turn their back on the earlier generation of "native" landscape painters, such as Salomon van Ruysdael. In this sense, they return to the tradition of Claude. They reintegrated Dutch culture with an aristocratic manner that the English later adopted in their gardens and that we Americans still later adopted, ironically, in our *public* parks.

——

In the seventeenth century, painting fully recognized landscape as a primary subject. But what does *landscape* mean? According to Edward Norgate in his *Miniatura,* written in the late 1640s, "nothing but a picture of Gle belle Vedute, or beautiful prospect of Fields,

Cities, Rivers, Castles, Mountains, Trees or whatsoever delightful view the Eye takes pleasure in, nothing more in Art or Nature affording soe great variety and beautie as beholding the farre distant Mountains and strange scituation of ancient Castles mounted on almost inaccessible Rocks."[29] In other words, a landscape is a good view. In the seventeenth century, the conception of a good view was formed and shared by the small group of people who made and purchased paintings. This process of conceptualizing the landscape was therefore similar to that which had occurred centuries earlier when the idea of a paradise or of an ideal human form had also been agreed upon. Its significance can hardly be overestimated, for it has molded our most basic scenic habits and taught us how to see. Since then we have all learned to recognize a good view.

These "good views" in seventeenth-century paintings are in and of themselves of such importance that they are no longer obliged to support some theme other than landscape. Foreground action, like the narrative themes it supported, is either nonexistent or reduced to decoration; it has been replaced by broader and deeper views—landscapes composed pictorially. Since these views were broader, they required for their execution a new convention, the "landscape-shaped," or horizontal, format. Landscape painting was so directly associated with wide views that the word *landscape* was even used to denote any oblong painting (as opposed to an upright-shaped one), whether or not it included any views we might consider landscape.[30]

The wide, horizontal format was joined with perspective techniques for creating depth. In the seventeenth century, the spectator's gaze was led diagonally across the landscape to the distance. Symmetry and centrality were abandoned. Irregular balance replaced the mirrored halves that had led to landscapes in the background of early Renaissance paintings. Such "natural carelessness"—what was later called "irregularity"—became a most significant compositional convention in the eighteenth century, and we still depend upon it.

It should not be too surprising, then, to find that late in the seventeenth century there were indications of the imminent popularity of actual, irregular landscapes. Wild and mountainous landscapes would soon be appreciated. Pictures themselves spread these ideas to England. We shall now look at actual landscapes whose very design was derived from the visual model that pictures—such as those we have just discussed—had provided. We are about to turn to the eighteenth-century English landscape garden, the pivotal development in the pictorialization of the landscape.

Picturesque Vision | II

Spectators of the Picturesque: Eighteenth-Century England

9

The two intimately related questions that initiated our inquiry—how did nature become pictorialized, and how did the landscape become interpreted as nature?—will now take us to England. Unlike the previous chapters, the focus here will not be on paintings themselves; instead, it will be on the revolutionary effects that the paintings we have already studied had on both the perception, and the actual design, of the landscape.

Following the artistic pinnacle of naturalistic landscape painting in the seventeenth century came the appreciation of actual landscape. Not only painting but also poetry, travel, gardening, and architecture were described as the single "art of landscape"[1] because they all stressed the role of landscape in stimulating the eye and, more importantly, the imagination.

This art of landscape was directly associated with the "picturesque" movement, since pictures, which manifested the artist's skills of observation, were taken as a guide for how to see. Early in the eighteenth century, *picturesque* could have been defined as "in the style of a picture." But by the beginning of the nineteenth century, the picturesque connoted not simply a style of composition but, as we shall see, an entirely new way of seeing. It not only revolutionized the form of the garden but also extended the idea of garden to the entire landscape itself.

An important commentator on this subject is Christopher Hussey. In *The Picturesque: Studies in a Point of View*, he describes a realization that he had about his own way of seeing. He recalls sitting in the library of his family home as a young boy, looking out the window at a perfectly composed English scene. He reached for a book by Uvedale Price that his grandfather had read. Browsing, he discovered that his grandfather had applied conventions learned from pictures to the siting of the house, the planting of the garden, and even the view out the window:

And before I read far, I reflected that all those scenes which I instinctively called artistic must be "picturesque," and that I was not being original when I sketched a hovel under a gnarled oak but appallingly traditional—the man wrote in 1794! . . . It was humiliating, at the time, to find my aesthetic impulses no more than a product of heredity and environment. Yet, it is gratifying to know the name of one's subjectivity. Though the knowledge killed my direct relish of the picturesque, I soon began to appreciate it consciously, *en vertuose*, disentangling its derivations, and marking its effect on the arts of two centuries. It gradually revealed itself as a long phase in the aesthetic relationship of man to nature.[2]

Without knowing it, Hussey had been seeing the world through principles developed in the eighteenth century. I suggest that this is precisely what we, even in the late twentieth century, still do. The eighteenth century remains the primary source for landscape design that echoes a pictorialized nature.

When English landowners had learned to see the way painters saw, they wanted the views from the windows of their estates to look like pictures. Furthermore, they even began to apply to landscapes that had not been designed as gardens the same criteria with which they had learned to judge paintings. The consequence of this was revolutionary: "nature" and the garden traded places. The garden came to look like the nature depicted by painters such as Claude and Rosa: irregular and full of variety. This garden was an illusion of nature, for this was a nature designed, bounded, and kept—an enclave surrounding the residence and called "the landscape garden." In an (almost) ironic twist, the land beyond the landscape garden was increasingly treated as the garden always had been: as an object of beauty. Adjacent agricultural fields, natural areas such as glens and bogs, and even towns themselves were judged by the same visual criteria that had been used to evaluate paintings and gardens. A comprehensive set of expectations thus developed: the landscape, whether within or beyond the garden, should be scenic.

In this chapter, we shall join Christopher Hussey in following a lengthy path through the eighteenth century in order to get a sense of its broad implications for landscape architecture. Now it is our turn to learn to name our own subjectivity.

Travel

Today we assume that an appreciation of the landscape as "scenery" has always existed. Yet as we have witnessed in the history of painting, the observation of landscape comes very late in the development of the Western mind.[3] We might recall the ancient Greeks' treatment of mountains and valleys as sacred, but that was many, many centuries ago and was followed for a thousand years by the idea, expressed best by Saint Anselm, that things were harmful in proportion to the number of senses they delighted. The idea of forests, mountains, and rivers as not only bewildering but also sinful lingered well into the seventeenth and early eighteenth centuries.

By the middle of the eighteenth century, however, such fear, repulsion, and distaste had virtually disappeared. As a quick glance at the reverent looks on the faces of today's tourists as they confront the prospect of the Rocky Mountains will testify, such feelings have not returned since. Indeed, it is hard to believe that such reverential seeing has not always existed. But as we have so often discussed, seeing is culturally based. In this case, the awakening of eighteenth-century England to the appreciation of landscape was a direct result of seeing Italian landscape paintings. The trip to Italy, which was an educational staple of the aristocracy, was known as "the Grand Tour," and the travelers who went on the Grand Tour wanted to see the landscapes that had produced the ancient and Renaissance cultures they admired so greatly. Ancient sculpture, Renaissance architecture, and the then-current landscape paintings were the significant artifacts. Today American students take European tours, which are often primarily shopping trips. The eighteenth-century aristocrats shopped too—for landscape paintings.

In their diaries, travelers on the Grand Tour described the visual effects in the landscapes they were visiting. They wrote, for example, about the stillness of the air, the strong lights and shades, the tints upon the mountains, and the polish of the lake. These are quite novel descriptions since, unlike their predecessors, these travelers did not emphasize the actual objects they were seeing. It is clear, therefore, that they were influenced by painting, for why else would they talk about such visual effects as "strong shades" or the "polish" on the lake? Although this language of seeing is quite familiar to us today, these descriptions are freshly seen and follow trips to Rome, where the travelers had viewed pictures by Claude and Rosa.[4] Quite simply, noting such visual effects in actual places was a new experience, one that had been formed by a knowledge of painting.

Two specific visual qualities attained prominence in the eighteenth century: vagueness and distance. Before that time, looking at distance only meant not seeing very clearly or very well. Today we are used to, though still somewhat titillated by, seeing great distances from airplanes or tall buildings. The fascination with this type of visual experience dates back only to the middle of the seventeenth century. Since that was a time bereft of airplanes and skyscrapers, the source of such visual experiences was not an actual place. Instead, it was Italian landscape painting, which culminated the development of pictorialization that had begun centuries earlier. By the end of the eighteenth century, the English were totally converted, and Gilpin could state, "Tis distance lends enchantment to the view."[5]

Crossing the Alps to get to Italy required tiresome effort with little reward. Joseph Addison's disgust for crossing the mountains and his relief upon seeing a plain was typical. However, on his return trip, after visiting Rome and seeing landscape paintings, Addison's opinion was changed. He appreciated "huge Precipices of naked Rocks . . . cleft in some places so as to discover high mountains of snow." At Albano, near Rome, he described a Claudian, amphitheatrical prospect and noted that "painters often work upon this Landskip."[6] In fact, after the English traveler had seen landscape paintings, the supreme experience of the Tour then became the rugged but visually exciting return trip across the Alps.

Mountains were only one of the many landscape features that became favorites for travelers' restless eyes. Typical eighteenth-century spectators were proficient in the art of what has been called "scene hopping"—traveling to places where they could see many grand prospects without wasting time either looking at details or journeying to several locations. In scene hopping, "we encounter a visual restlessness and lack of concentration, a somewhat distracted wandering of the eye, legitimized as a submission to nature's seemingly infinite variety and breadth."[7] Today we are quite familiar with such visual restlessness. Our eyes have become accustomed to the constant flicker of electronic dots, and we feel the need to change scenes about every twelve minutes—the time span between television commercials. In the eighteenth century, however, the need for changing scenes was something quite new. Spectators had seen many views in paintings by Claude and Rosa. "These paintings provided, above all, a sense of nature's variety, . . . Variety became in turn the central criterion of the landscape gardener."[8] Of course, nature had not suddenly changed. Human nature, or rather, specific individuals who had been exposed to paintings, had developed a new need for visual variety.

During the passage across the Alps and the journey through Italy, English travelers not only consumed a variety of landscapes—they also bought them. This appreciation for "scenery" coincided with the emergence of a new social type, the connoisseur or educated collector. While on their Grand Tours, English travelers purchased landscape paintings and brought these souvenirs home, where they were hung on the walls next to windows that looked out at Dutch- and French-style gardens. The contrast was disconcerting, and by the middle of the eighteenth century the view out the window would be composed to look like nature as represented in paintings.

From the experiences of seeing both paintings and landscapes, English spectators had learned to see the landscape as a composition. "The contemplation of landscape was an activity with its own proper procedure, which involved recognising the stretch of land under your eye not, simply, as that—as an area of ground filled with various objects, trees, hills, fields—but as a complex of associations and meanings, and, more important, as a composition, in which each object bore a specific and analysable relationship to the others. This recognition of the formal structure of a landscape was not a purely passive activity—a considerable amount of jockeying for position, of screwing up the eyes, of moving back and forth, of rearranging objects in the imagination, had to be gone through before a view came right."[9] This should sound familiar. It should remind us of our own jockeying for position and borrowing of trees to frame views when we take pictures. We do this not simply because we have learned a technique for picture taking but also because of a deeply ingrained habit of seeing which is based on the compositional conventions that constitute a view.

Imagined Pictures

The idea of imagining paintings as a result of reading literature was reinvigorated in eighteenth-century England. For example, Alexander Pope wrote this note about Homer's *Iliad*: "I cannot conclude the Notes to this Book without observing, that what seems the principal Beauty of it, and what distinguishes it among all the others, is the Liveliness of its Paintings."[10] Even though the *Iliad* had been written in the eighth century B.C.E., Pope found it filled with "paintings." Obviously, he had a lively imagination, one that was thoroughly informed by the picturesque sensibility of the day.

Much discussion was centered on sight and its relationship to the imagination. One of the leaders of the debate was Joseph Addison, who wrote in the *Spectator* in 1712 an essay entitled "Pleasures of the Imagination." Referring to John Locke's *Essay Concerning Human Under-standing* (1690), Addison states, "I have here supposed that my reader is ac-quainted with that great modern discovery which is at present universally acknowledged by all the enquirers into natural philosophy; namely, that light and colors, as apprehended by the imagination, are only ideas in the mind and not qualities that have any existence in matter."[11] Locke had given authority to individual experience and distinguished the individual's imagination from the world outside. In keeping with this notion, Addison, who relied entirely on sight as the source of all imagination, therefore encouraged "individual freedom" in seeing.

The Mind of Man naturally hates every thing that looks like a Restraint upon it, and is apt to fancy it self under a sort of confinement, when the Sight is pent up in a narrow Compass, and shortned on every side by the Neighbourhood of Walls or Mountains. On the contrary, a spacious Horison is an Image of Liberty, where the Eye has Room to range abroad, to expatiate at large on the Immensity of its Views, and to lose it self amidst the

Variety of Objects that offer themselves to its Observation. Such wide and undetermined Prospects are as pleasing to the Fancy, as the Speculations of Eternity or Infinitude are to the Understanding.[12]

Addison succeeded in praising, and uniting, both liberty (and thereby England in its ascendency in the political arena) and broad views of landscape.[13] The consequence of opening up the landscape so that one's sight could wander was that garden walls, which had for centuries indicated the limits of design, would be entirely removed. The landscape itself would be seen in terms of the pleasure and profit it could provide:

> But why may not a whole estate be thrown into a kind of garden by frequent plantations, that may turn as much to the profit as the pleasure of the owner? . . . Fields of corn make a pleasant prospect and, if the walks were a little taken care of that lie between them, if the natural embroidery of the meadows were helped and improved by some small additions of art, and the several rows of hedges set off by trees and flowers that the soil was capable of receiving, a man might make a pretty landskip of his own possessions.[14]

It must be remembered that at this time *landskip* simply denoted a type of painting. Addison's use of this word to describe an actual place demonstrates clearly that paintings came to mind when an eighteenth-century connoisseur used his imagination to contemplate great images.

This elevation of the pictorial imagination was taken up as a theme for poetry. Indeed, Thomson, Dyer, and their immediate followers are usually designated the Landscape Poets.[15] Poets of all generations have described landscape at some time or another, but these poets looked at and described landscape in terms of pictures. The reason is clear: Dyer and Thomson had something earlier poets had not had—landscapes, abundantly multiplied in painting and print, by Claude and other landscape painters.[16]

Before 1730 the word *picturesque* had not yet become associated with landscape. That year, Dyer's "Grongar Hill" and Thomson's *Seasons* were published, and a major step toward picturesque vision was thereby taken.[17] These poets' achievement was to teach the well-read men and women of England a visual appreciation similar to that which had been felt for the Italian landscape painters. They taught their readers to imagine a series of more or less well-composed landscape pictures:

> Ever charming, ever new
> When will the landscape tire the view!
> The fountain's fall, the river's flow,

> The woody vallies, warm and low,
> The windy summits, wild and high,
> Roughly rushing on the sky!
> The pleasant seat, the ruin'd tow'r,
> The naked rock, the shady bow'r,
> The town, the village, dome and farm. . . .[18]

Almost every line forces the reader to visualize a painterly scene. Both Claude and Rosa are referred to "in James Thomson's *Castle of Indolence* [1748], where a colourful, rural, natural and atmospheric scene is said to contain 'Whate'er Lorrain light-touched with softening hue, Or savage Rosa dashed, or learned Poussin drew.'"[19]

Literature had succeeded, during the first half of the eighteenth century, in reinforcing landscape imaging and in discovering the delight visual images produced. The stage was set for the development of the landscape garden. There were connoisseurs who owned large estates and imported landscape paintings; and aristocrats had become devoted to the power of the imagination. An appreciation of "scenery" prevailed. Now was the time to go beyond merely thinking of or imagining landscape in pictorial terms: it was time to transform the land into a picture.

Early Landscape Gardens

An important aspect of the Grand Tours, many seventeenth-century landscape paintings, and newly translated ancient texts was the renewed access they provided to classical themes. Not surprisingly, a key source of classical themes was the Virgilian pastoral. Eighteenth-century estate owners must have realized that Virgil's description of the rural dwelling could not be truly represented by the embroidered flowerbeds and axial garden design whose forms they had inherited from Dutch and French sources. For this reason, and also because the English of that time were vigorously repudiating French authority in the arts and politics, existing gardens were therefore rejected, and a new visual model was sought. Because Virgil had not made drawings for the English to copy, paintings by Claude and Poussin (created seventeen hundred years after Virgil) were taken as reliable illustrations of what Virgil had meant.[20] Robert Castell's translation of Pliny the Younger's letters describing villas near Rome confirmed and promoted the compositions provided by the painters. Castell's demonstration that the temples and other structures that dotted the landscape in Claude's pictures were indeed consistent with Roman ideas helped English connoisseurs to reproduce on their own soil their images of ancient landscapes. Castell named three "styles" of Roman garden design: (a) the plain and unadorned; (b) the "regular," laid out "by the Rule and Line"; and (c) the imitation of rural landscapes, or the *Imitatio Ruris*, where

> the form of a beautiful Country, Hills, Rocks, Cascades, Rivulets, Woods, Buildings, & c. were possibly thrown into such an agreeable Disorder, as to have pleased the Eye for several Views, like so many beautiful Landskips; and at the same time have afforded at least all of the pleasures that could be enjoy'd in the most regular Gardens. . . . a close Imitation of Nature; where, tho' the Parts are disposed with the greatest Art, the Irregularity is still preserved; so that their Manner may not improperly be said to be an artful Confusion, where there is no Appearance of that Skill which is made use of, their Rocks, Cascades, and Trees, bearing their natural Forms.[21]

In this one quote we find the remaining ingredients for the landscape garden: "agreeable Disorder" or "artful Confusion," apparent oxymorons that reveal some of the difficulty of designing a representation of a rural landscape; views that please the eye "like so many beautiful Landskips," in other words, views that look like paintings; an illusion of nature so skillfully rendered that one cannot detect that it was designed; and most important, all of it disposed irregularly.

Irregularity itself was, and still is, associated with nature.[22] Today, almost anything, from a house to a path is considered more "natural" when turned slightly askew than when aligned. A curve, perhaps even a regularly geometric one, is considered more natural than a straight line. Indeed, irregularity has become as conventional as symmetry ever was. Just because a landscape seems irregular when we look out across a wide expanse does not mean that nature, too, is irregular, unless we also think of nature simply as a view. The eighteenth century's concern for irregularity, as well as our own, is paradigmatic not of a new discovery in natural science but of a new pictorial sensibility, for as pleasing as irregularity may be, an irregular design is anything but natural.

CASTLE HOWARD

One of the best examples of how Castell's characterization of Roman garden design affected contemporary design is Castle Howard, by Sir John Vanbrugh, begun in 1701 (fig. 9.1). There, Vanbrugh detached the classical building from the authoritative straight line of its avenue approach. "As a stage designer, Vanbrugh must have experienced the art of creating idyllic imaginary space within a small compass. Here, he is practising on a great scale. The mansion stands in the centre of the scenery and its tenuous attachment to the avenue is an early suggestion, developed later in the century, that a house should be entirely cut off from the outside world. The stage all around was vast

Fig. 9.1. Castle Howard, Yorkshire. Photograph by Robert Harvey.

Fig. 9.2. Claude Lorrain, *Landscape near Rome with a View of the Ponte Molle* (1645). Birmingham Museum and Art Gallery, Birmingham, England.

and the scenery like some Arcadian landscape organized according to the character of the natural landscape."[23] The design of this early landscape garden is composed to emulate a natural landscape, although we do not know which one. Cutting the garden off from the existing landscape is crucial to the success of this ploy. Castle Howard's connection to its surroundings is intentionally broken; the castle stands as an enclave, its landscape garden quite unlike a natural landscape. Or, to use a critical term, the castle is "framed" in precisely the same manner as a painting.

Furthermore, the architect invoked in his design for Castle Howard three of the most famous ingredients of a painting by Claude, *Landscape near Rome with a View of the Ponte Molle* (fig. 9.2). In a recent picture of Castle Howard (fig. 9.1), a round building, the Mausoleum, and a Palladian bridge are seen from a square building, the Temple of the Four Winds; in Claude's painting we see a square and a round building and a Palladian bridge. The prospect composed by these three elements is one of the grandest of ideal Claudian landscapes ever to be created.[24]

PAINSHILL

There are other examples of landscape designs that were direct imitations of seventeenth-century painters' works. William Gilpin's sketch of Painshill (fig. 9.3); looks west from the Gothic temple to the Temple of Bacchus, a Palladian bridge, and a tower in the treeline. Part of the lakeside, shown as seen today in figure 9.4, is known to have been modeled on some Rosa sketches.[25] "Later writers who described Painshill—Uvedale Price, for example—said that Hamilton [its owner and designer, who lived there for more than thirty years after 1738] had studied Italian painters in designing his garden, and that the spirit of Salvator Rosa was evoked with particular success. This spirit, unlike the glowing and peaceful evocation of Arcadian beauty in Claude, was one of wildness and gloom: "savage" and "impetuous" are adjectives which the century attached to Rosa's art. At Painshill, this came no doubt from the "Gothic" buildings, but more from the extensive plantings of conifers (said in 1781 to be the most varied collection in the world) and from the famous and "primitive" grotto works which looked out over the lake."[26] We can imagine dark and foreboding spaces in the grotto, which was formed by dense plantings of evergreens, seemingly uninhabited and beyond society's rules.

STOURHEAD

The finest example of a garden that provides viewers with "pictures" in the landscape is the "pictorial circuit" garden of Stourhead (1735–

Fig. 9.3. Painshill, Surrey, sketch by William Gilpin (1772). Courtesy of Mrs. Pamela Benson.

Fig. 9.4. Painshill, Surrey. Photograph by Robert Harvey.

83), built by its owner, Henry Hoare. The garden offers a series of shifting pictures with sight lines directed across a lake, terminating on small buildings scenically placed in the larger valley landscape. Stourhead is thoroughly allegorical: the monuments that terminate sight lines "tell" the story of Aeneas's visit to the underworld (as described in books 3 and 6 of Virgil's *Aeneid*).

Despite our almost total ignorance of Virgil, this garden still feels familiar to a casual twentieth-century observer. It is not now surprising to see a monument strategically placed on a sight line across a lake (although today instead of a miniature version of the Pantheon we might expect to see an IBM sign). Stourhead is one of the first gardens to maintain complete visual control by concealing its boundaries, extending them farther than a visitor can see. By doing this, it took another step toward becoming the landscape garden. Today, suburban corporations buy large areas of land to maintain just this kind of control of their image.

The Claudian feeling at Stourhead is intentional, as is made quickly evident by the close resemblance between a photograph of Stourhead (fig. 9.5) and Claude's *Coast View of Delos with Aeneas* (fig. 9.6). The Pantheon seems to be inspired by the temple in Claude's *View of Delphi with a Procession*, of which Hoare owned a version by another artist.[27] Stourhead's Temple of Apollo is placed on an elevation from which one could gain, according to Hussey, "before the side-screening trees encroached upon it, the most extensive view of the elysium, and the most beautiful, when from the spectators's left, evening light casts over it the appropriate Claudian glow."[28] In a letter to his daughter, Hoare claimed that "the view of the Bridge, Village and Church altogether will be a charming Gaspard (Poussin) picture at the end of that water."[29]

In these three gardens, we have seen paintings serve as models for garden "pictures." But in the first half of the eighteenth century, paintings served an even more important purpose than simply providing patterns, as we shall now see.

STOWE

We have seen from these gardens designed by their owners that the landscape garden did not appear suddenly as a weird idea of an individual designer. As Nikolas Pevsner has stated, the landscape garden "was conceived by philosophers, writers and virtuosi—not by architects and gardeners."[30] As a result, the English landscape garden was the product of a community of arts, implemented by a particular group of landowners who had the required background to execute the ideas that were being discussed in literature and art.

Most importantly, although it was deeply integrated with other arts, the revolutionary and pictorial form of the landscape garden

Fig. 9.5. Stourhead, Wiltshire. Photograph by Robert Harvey.

Fig. 9.6. Claude Lorrain, *Coast View of Delos with Aeneas*. National Gallery, London.

was itself a narrative and thus subservient to its subject matter.[31] This is crucial to remember. Not only is the English landscape garden—the paradigm of today's design—not natural, but in its original form it told a traditional—that is, culturally embedded—story.

We shall now look at Stowe, the most important landscape garden of the first half of the eighteenth century, in order to get a sense of the early landscape garden's pictorial and narrative structure. Richard Temple Cobham was the owner, and the professional team of designers were Charles Bridgeman, who determined its basic structure, John Vanbrugh, William Kent, and James Gibbs.

Although the gardens at Stowe evolved for nearly one hundred years, the modifications that were made in the 1730s are in striking contrast to the earlier garden. A plan view of the earlier garden looks like a defensive encampment dissected by straight lines diverging in all directions, full of slant views, triangular woods, curved paths, and various surprises. Its boundary is emphatically defined by lines of trees, positioned defensively. Even with such clear boundaries, this garden itself represented a radical departure from even earlier gardens, for it had broken with the time-honored principle of symmetry. The result is that existing site features, such as a road and a pond, were incorporated into the garden. This recognition that the landscape and the garden are *both* products of human design, and the consequent merger of the two, becomes essential to the very definition of landscape architecture.

In the 1730s a true landscape garden whose appearance is pastoral takes form; undulating openings intermingle with wooded areas. It is still a landscape: that is, it is designed by human beings. The transition from the linear geometry of the earlier garden to the serpentine irregularity of the latter has produced the appearance of an idyllic, safe, free, and comfortable place that needs no defense. But, like the pastoral oasis in which Tityrus resided and which Meliboeus was forced to leave, it is an illusion. Despite its intention to look otherwise, the latter version of Stowe is an enclave, designed by human beings and as defensively bounded as the earlier version.

Kent is one designer most credited with the conception of the landscape garden in the early eighteenth century. He was trained as a painter and was sent to Italy on the Grand Tour to attend the opera, draw, and acquire landscape paintings. In later years he owned originals or copies of paintings by Claude, Rosa, and Gaspard.[32] Kent's training in the theater and painting led him to design gardens that lead the spectator from one "picture" to another and have been described as "a continued series of new and delightful scenes at every step we take."[33] As we shall see, these pictures were not simply compositions to be viewed. Like the Italian landscape paintings upon which they were modeled, they were to be understood with reference to classical literature and contemporary culture.

The area at Stowe most closely associated with Kent is the valley of
the Elysian Fields,[34] where the Temple of Ancient Virtue is sited on
one bank and the Temple of British Worthies on the other. "One contemporary is recorded as saying that the 'Elysian Fields . . . is the
painting part of [Cobham's] gardens.'"[35] Indeed, the Elysian Fields
are designed as a pictorial and perspectival experience. The long and
winding valley is firmly Claudian, hidden from the main vista by
dense clumps of trees to enhance the appearance of depth. This is the
convention of coulisse, transferred from the stage to painting, perfected by Claude, now used in gardens.

The history of the Temple of Ancient Virtue not only includes
Claude but even goes back to the first century. A classical building, it
was probably modeled after the so-called Temple of Sybil set above
the gorge at Tivoli (which had itself already become a garden orna-
ment in antiquity when Hadrian created a garden around it at his
villa). Claude, in the seventeenth century, drew or painted the Temple
of Sybil more than forty times. A century later, Kent copied it for
Stowe. After being pictured so extensively, the Temple of Sybil then
became the most frequently imitated ancient building. Twenty or
more versions were built in the British Isles, and as many more on
the continent.

The temples in the Elysian Fields were sited by Kent so that they
could be seen perfectly "pictured" in the water before they were
reached. What was the source of this idea? Seventeenth-century painting. Movement was a crucial characteristic of the baroque painting
that had reached England at the same time that the picturesque point
of view was forming. Consequently, landscape designers tried to incorporate the idea of movement into the landscape garden at the
same time they were incorporating other pictorial devices.

In painting, the rise and fall, advance and recess, and convexity
and concavity of form has the same effect of creating movement as do
hill and dale, foreground and distance, and swelling and sinking in
the landscape. For the spectator in an actual landscape, however, topographic relief does more than affect the eyes; it necessitates bodily
movement as well. More importantly, it creates a distinction between
the eyes and feet and becomes the design principle that mandates that
the foot should never travel by the same route as the eye. The eyes
can travel quickly, "irritated" by lights and shades, while the feet
stroll leisurely over hill and dale. Today we are quite familiar with
this design principle: the path the eye follows to identify a landmark
is different than that traveled by car.

As stated earlier, the design of the Elysian Fields discloses more
than the formal conventions inherited from painting. It is also allegorical: it is a landscape of symbols in a progression which is intended to communicate a truth about human existence. It is this
sense of narrative that early eighteenth-century gardens shared with

painting and drama. If the spectators of the Elysian Fields are learned and witty (and Whigs), the design yields a full and intricate narrative in which they are necessarily involved.

The Temple of Ancient Virtue contained within its structure four full-length statues of exemplary ancients. Nearby existed, in the early eighteenth century, a satirically built ruin, the Temple of Modern Virtue. To be encountered across what was called the River Styx was the Temple of British Worthies, which contained sixteen elaborately inscribed busts of notable Britons. The oval niche in the pyramid of the temple contained a head of Mercury, the messenger god who leads the souls of heroes to the Elysian Fields. "The meanings of this triangular arrangement are appreciated by the garden visitor largely through perspective, an essentially pictorial structure of their action in which form and content cooperate."[36]

But one would wonder how much of the narrative could be interpreted by today's visitor. Would we recognize the Temple of Ancient Virtue from paintings by Claude? Might we identify with a deliberately ruined Temple of Modern Virtue across from the ancient one? Our modern lack of understanding of Stowe's narrative might well make us see Stowe's garden simply as a familiar form that we would too casually label "natural."

In addition to its references to ancient literature, Stowe's design also made political comments. For example, the deliberately decayed Temple of Modern Virtue represented the decay of the Tory government as viewed by the Whigs. More specifically, the headless statue in that temple represented a political opponent of Lord Cobham's, Sir Robert Walpole. In a more general sense, the landscape garden's forms were presented as a political challenge to the brash, worldly, and authoritarian attitudes that the English attributed to the axial and geometric French gardens.[37] The English landscape garden was taken to be more natural because it was rooted in a democracy.

To summarize: the English landscape garden of the first half of the eighteenth century as exemplified by Stowe, is thoroughly laden with cultural significance. Even though it is curving and irregular, it is no more natural than a French rectangle. The opportunity for undirected movement, which resulted from the break with geometry, represented openness and freedom to the garden's English owners. This appearance, however, is the consequence of design and calculated manipulation. The extraordinary appeal of this design in American landscape architecture is surely a result of the fact that the landscape garden's potential for undirected movement feels like and looks like, freedom. The success of the English landscape garden can be measured by the extent to which it has concealed its own artifice and caused us to forget the fact that this opportunity for undirected movement is the consequence of the highly directed thought of the English aristocracy.

The Landscape Garden in
the Second Half of the Century

*Spectators
of the
Picturesque*

127

In the middle of the eighteenth century, English intellectuals became particularly interested in questions of form. In fact, "a person of much education in the eighteenth century would have found it very hard, not merely to describe land, but also to see it, and even to *think* of it as a visual phenomenon, except as mediated through particular notions of form. The words 'landscape,' 'scene,' and, to a lesser extent, 'prospect,' demanded, in short, that the land be thought of as itself composed into the formal patterns which previously a landscape painter would have been thought of as himself imposing on it."[38] In other words, the landscape spectators of the eighteenth century had so thoroughly incorporated the ideas of form from painters that the actual landscape they saw could not be separated from formal painting conventions. As a result, they wanted to know why the painter's model worked so well. They wondered about exactly what kinds of forms produced delight. The result was a series of aesthetic arguments intended to answer these questions. Two of the most popular theories, put forth in Edmund Burke's *A Philosophical Enquiry into the Origin of Our Ideas of the Sublime and Beautiful* (1756), and William Hogarth's *The Analysis of Beauty* (1753), respectively, argued that particular forms, in and of themselves, were beautiful.

It is no coincidence that Capability Brown's landscape garden, which defined the landscape garden of the second half of the century and upon whose forms we still depend, came into being in the same decade that these two theories were disseminated. The concurrence of these theories with Brown's work suggests that, at a minimum, he was influenced by these two books. This is certainly the case with other earlier designers such as William Shenstone in his work at the Leasowes. However, Brown's "conception of landscape represents so exactly Burke's of 'Beauty,' and made such notorious use of Hogarth's serpentine 'line of beauty'"[39] that we need to understand Burke's and Hogarth's conception of beauty in order to understand Brown's landscape garden.

Hogarth's *Analysis of Beauty* identifies serpentine lines as the highest form of beauty. Despite the fact that it no longer carries weight as a visual theory, Hogarth's work remains crucial to our story. The serpentine line he championed so enthusiastically is still defended today as somehow "natural." Hogarth describes it as reflective of a life of leisure.[40] He uses woman's body as the most exact proof that the serpentine line is the highest form of beauty.[41] While it might seem an honorable distinction for women to represent the highest form of beauty, in fact, Hogarth has trivialized women by implying that they are ornamental objects to be enjoyed at men's leisure.

Hogarth also based his arguments on ethnocentric distinctions. He argued, for example, that the minuet, a dance of the upper classes, was based on serpentine movement, while "the dances of barbarians are always represented without these movements, being only composed of wild skipping, jumping, and turning around, or running backward and forward, with convulsive shrugs, and distorted gestures."[42] If Hogarth's judgment about the most beautiful form of movement is transferred from dance to design, the landscape garden is clearly meant to be the garden of the minuet.

Burke believed that objects were perceived directly by the senses and, like the lines in Hogarth's theory, had innate qualities that aroused particular responses in spectators. He divided visual objects into two basic categories: the beautiful and the sublime. The latter was characterized by vastness, infinitude, magnificence, power, and obscurity. After the publication of Burke's *Enquiry*, Salvator Rosa's name became almost synonymous with the word *sublime*, as applied to the landscape.[43] Indeed, after seeing Rosa's paintings people looked appreciatively at rugged places as they never had before.

The qualities of the beautiful, on the other hand, were defined by Burke as smallness, smoothness, delicacy, and gradual variation. Like Hogarth, Burke associated the qualities he considered beautiful with women. Also like Hogarth, Burke by means of his theories gave form to the landscape garden. The landscape garden was to be designed to represent a beautiful "nature," particularly those aspects of nature that were perceived by, and gave pleasure to, a particular group of eighteenth-century men.

This discussion of form as an introduction to Capability Brown's work might seem out of place. The landscape garden is, after all famous precisely for being informal. At least, *informal* is the term that garden history books have traditionally used in describing the landscape garden, and even today, on the licensing exam for landscape architects, "informal" is a correct answer to a question about how to describe an amebic form (like one of Brown's lakes). But *informal* cannot really describe form, since its own prefix negates it. What *informal* more accurately describes is behavior: casual, without ceremony, open to individual choice; the behavior of the stroller walking across the designed and mown meadow of a landscape garden or today's park.

However informal the behavior it recommends, the landscape garden is for several reasons decidedly formal. First, eighteenth-century landscape gardeners relied upon the same kind of formal balance used by painters. The French and Dutch gardens that preceded the landscape garden are typically described as "formal," for their balance relied upon parts mirroring parts, or symmetry. Similarly, the landscape garden relies upon parts balanced by other parts, or coordination, in the manner we described above when discussing the composition of Claude's paintings. Both types of gardens, therefore, adhere to clearly defined formal principles that can be observed. A ninety-degree angle is as out of place in a landscape garden for example, as a serpentine line would be at Versailles. This does not imply, however, that the former is any less formal than the latter. But there is a more significant sense in which Brown's landscape garden is formal: it uses form alone to articulate meaning. In the garden at Stowe, we saw how content and form had been integrated into the garden. But Brown's landscape garden, like the aesthetic theories of Burke and Hogarth, assumes that forms themselves have inherent meanings.

What separated Brown from earlier designers who also understood these theories is that he neglected mottoes and inscriptions, statues and incidental buildings; he swept the lawn straight up to the walls of the house and thus eliminated specific gardens in order to give the building the appearance of being planted in the park.[44] The scene is not dominated by bizarre follies or grottoes, and there are no abrupt contrasts to create any kind of surprise. Brown thus banished from the garden the words and objects that had formerly provided the references for its visitors. He designed "scenery" that was dramatic not in the sense of creating associations and evoking emotions, but only in its compositional form.

Brown summed up an ideal through his selection of a representative form: the serpentine line discussed by Hogarth as the line of beauty. Price said of Brown, "He is the very emblem of serpentine walks, belts, and rivers, and all Mr. Brown's works—like him they are smooth, flowing, even and distinct—and like him they wear one's soul out."[45] Brown's generalized forms were composed to elicit very general ideas in the minds of spectators. Everyone knew the game. For example, undirected movement in meandering open spaces meant freedom and individual choice, while the function of water in a spacious lake was to allow the mind to expand itself in great ideas and to delight in vastness.

Indeed, the gardens themselves were vast. Landowners, after 1750, could afford such extravagant gardens mainly because of the parliamentary enclosure acts that authorized the fencing of open fields and abolished common rights to the fields.[46] Landowners consolidated their property into large single blocks of land with the house and its park at the center and shelter belts at its edge, and they hired back dispossessed peasants to work the newly enclosed ground.

Unlike the early landscape gardens, Brown's parks were not calculated to stimulate philosophical or historical reflections. He succeeded, however, in enshrining an ideal image of the Virgilian pastoral. To do so he followed the lead of the painters who had eliminated or reduced to shadows ploughed fields, cowsheds, kitchen gardens. One reason Brown's garden came be thought of as natural is because it disguised all evidence of toil. The rectangular fields of the enclosure movement were no longer to be seen. "As the real landscape began to look increasingly artifical, like a garden, the garden began to look increasingly natural, like the pre-enclosed landscape. Thus a natural landscape became the prerogative of the estate, allowing for a conveniently ambiguous signification, so that nature was the sign of property and property the sign of nature. . . . Its delicately serpentined stream and undulating grassy hills evoke the estate as a state of nature."[47]

This is the pivotal moment in the pictorialization of nature: what is designed (and owned) is composed to give the illusion of being natural, when in fact it is maintained as an enclave. To create the illusion, Brown's garden used compositional conventions taken from painting, but did not echo painting's use of literary themes. Earlier in the century, the imitation of nature (to a poet such as Dryden) had meant human nature.[48] Increasingly it meant something visual: a forested landscape with serpentine clearings.

"Simultaneously, Nature, with its various representations in painting, poetry, letters, manners, dress, philosophy and science, became a supreme social value and was called upon to clarify and justify social change. One now did something in a certain way because it was more 'natural'; one said something in a certain way because it sounded more 'natural'; something worked as it did because it was its 'nature' to do so. In the eighteenth and nineteenth centuries almost all change was accommodated under the rubric of 'nature' and 'naturalness.'"[49]

All previous gardens had maintained a clear distinction between themselves and either "art" or "nature." The landscape garden, however, tended to collapse the distinctions. To borrow a term from painting, it became a trompe l'oeil.[50] Brown's landscape garden disguised the boundaries that made it an enclave. The garden was surrounded by landscape, but for the first time, that which looked cultivated lay outside, and that which looked (spuriously) natural lay inside.

This was a new sensibility, one that spoke directly to its surroundings and privately to its spectators. Such was the goal of creating a "natural" garden. Brown's garden, however, spoke to its surroundings not by being native but by creating an ideal "nature." This freedom from direction was taken up and extended by American landscape designers, who simply provided the condition for private contemplation: a composed pastoral setting vaguely associated with democracy.

In the work of Humphrey Repton (figs. 9.7 and 9.8), Brown's successor, we come full circle: a landscape designer paints a picture of an actual place based on all the pictorial conventions that originally led to the creation of the landscape garden. In his "Red Books," Repton illustrated his proposals for improving country seats and parks in a series of eye-catching watercolors accompanied by text. A picture of

Fig. 9.7. Number 5 Attingham Park in Shropshire. From Humphrey Repton, *The Red Books of Humphrey Repton,* vol. 3.

Fig. 9.8. Number 5 Attingham Park in Shropshire. From Humphrey Repton, *The Red Books of Humphrey Repton,* vol. 3.

the proposed modifications would often be fitted with a flap that bore a picture of the existing site. When the flap was lifted, the proposed modifications would be revealed. This practical device is a classic instance of a landscape designer's use of a pictorial approach that employs the familiar conventions of painting: a singular location for the viewer, a large, distant view.

Picturesque Vision

Late in the eighteenth century, the landscape garden was criticized both for differing very little from common fields and for imitating too closely dull and vulgar nature.[51] The very characteristic that made it so widely popular, the elimination of ideas, was, ironically, also the reason it lacked definition. Those who sought wilder scenery than the English country estate deserted the garden and followed picturesque tours into the English countryside. These connoisseurs had learned a great deal about judging beauty, first from paintings and then from the landscape garden. Now they were leaving the garden to view the landscape. Touring England became the craze. "To read in sequence the published travel writings of those who undertook to explore the curiosities of their own country during the eighteenth century is to register not only the extraordinary amount of gardening carried out, but the steady spread of landscaping taste throughout the British Isles."[52] Between 1740 and 1840 there were no less than thirty one editions of guides to Stowe.[53] The passion for visually informed touring and its attendant activity, landscape sketching (today replaced by photography), was led by William Gilpin. He analyzed landscapes, such as rivers, the Highlands and the Lake District, in terms of the effects created by seventeenth-century painters. The picturesque travelers had a conception of an ideal form of nature, derived from landscape painting, and they aimed to discover ideal scenes in actual places. Not that the travelers often succeeded, but as Gilpin put it, it "amused" them to try.

Gilpin's influence on landscape architecture is shown by Frederick Law Olmsted's comments on Gilpin's work. Olmsted urged his employees to read Gilpin's published works because he valued them "so much more than any published since, as stimulating the exercise of judgment in matters of my art, that I put them into the hands of my pupils as soon as they come into our office saying, 'You are to read these seriously, as a student of law would read Blackstone.'"[54]

Gilpin's practical advice is instructive, contributing to an understanding not only of the late eighteenth century but also of the development of our own scenic habits. For example, Gilpin would say: "The whole view was pleasing from various stands: but to make it particularly picturesque by gaining a good foreground, we were

obliged to change our station backward & forward, till we had obtained a good one. Two large plane trees, which we met with, were of
great assistance to us."[55] The foreground tree is one of the most familiar conventions for framing scenes, first in paintings, then in architectural drawings. Now we place it in the upper corners of our
viewfinders to provide picturesque touches to our Kodak prints.

———

By 1780 an English school of landscape painters had joined the poets
and travelers in celebrating English scenery. Gainsborough, though
he employed pictorial conventions from Italian and Dutch masters,
selected typically English scenes and saw them from an English point
of view, and thus gave his pictures a native stamp. The English landscape could finally be compared to, and found to closely resemble, an
English landscape painting rather than an Italian one.

By the end of the eighteenth century, travel, which had once created astonishment as travelers encountered new landscapes, was reduced to creating mere acknowledgment as stories and pictures of
travel experiences became more common. This is easy for us to understand, for we are bombarded by pictures of the Grand Canyon
before we actually see it. Indeed, when we do arrive there, it looks
much like those pictures we've seen all our lives. This fall from astonishment to acknowledgment made some people question whether
the sights themselves motivated their responses. The discussion about
picturesque beauty in the second half of the eighteenth century piv-
oted around the actual relation of pictures to landscape experience.
Were picturesque landscapes simply those that looked like paintings?
How should picturesque landscapes be designed? Was the picturesque
a category separate from the sublime and the beautiful? If not, was
the picturesque a way of seeing—and, therefore, subjective—rather
than a quality inherent in objects?

This was the state of questioning at the end of the eighteenth century when Richard Payne Knight published *The Landscape* and Uvedale Price published *Essays on the Picturesque* (the very book Christopher Hussey picked up in his grandfather's library a century later).
Two illustrations from *The Landscape* show, first, how a landscape
would look if it were based on picturesque principles inherited from
painting (fig. 9.9), and then how it would look if Capability Brown
had designed it (fig. 9.10). Knight published these etchings to question whether Brown's landscape design was picturesque and to search
for an understanding of what the picturesque meant.

In fact, both compositions follow the same conventions: trees act
as coulisses framing the distant space that surrounds the estate
house; topographic bands, a winding river, and the diminution of
trees heighten the effect of perspective. Both compositions look familiar today because the basic compositional forms inherited from

Fig. 9.9. Etching by Hearne and Pouncy from Richard Payne Knight's *The Landscape* (1794). By permission of the Syndics of Cambridge University Library, Cambridge.

Fig. 9.10. Etching by Hearne and Pouncy from Richard Payne Knight's *The Landscape* (1794). By permission of the Syndics of Cambridge University Library, Cambridge.

painting remain. The first, however, looks like the typical low-maintenance scheme of our public parks; and the second, like the high-maintenance style typical of corporate headquarters: the ground plane has been tidied up. The differences are not in form but in detail.

In his *Analytical Inquiry into the Principles of Taste*, published a few years later, Knight insisted that nature has formed some of its own compositions in the style of painting and that the observer will learn from pictures to appreciate in nature "the picturesque parts: that is, those which nature has formed in the style and manner appropriate to painting; and the eye that has been accustomed to see these happily displayed and embellished by art, will relish them more in nature; as a person conversant with the writings of Theocritus and Virgil will relish pastoral scenery more than one unacquainted with such poetry."[56] This theory makes an education (in painting and literature) essential to the appreciation of "nature."

If what Knight says is true, one wonders today why the landscape garden is still so popular in parks and campuses when its users are not familiar with seventeenth-century landscape paintings, or why suburbia keeps trying to look pastoral when surely its inhabitants have not read Virgil. Even without knowing it, parks, campuses, corporate headquarters, and suburbs create associations to wealthy eighteenth-century estates whose owners, in the first half of that century, were themselves educated in art and literature. Such associations, even if not understood, are somehow felt; they have been sedimented under two centuries of acculturation, but their power is with us today.

It was Knight who first traced the origin of the term *picturesque* to the Italian *pittoresco* ("after the manner of painters").[57] He showed that it had first been used in reference to the painter Titian, a student of Giorgione (see fig. 7.1), and denoted the blending of objects into a kind of indistinctness. Therefore he argued that "abstract vision" was the painter's, or the picturesque, point of view. *The capacity for seeing (nature) with a painter's eye was picturesque vision.* Here Knight is arguing not simply that picturesque vision is the capacity to imitate paintings but that it requires learning to see the world the way painters have learned to see it.

Price, although a friend of Knight's, had quite a different point of view regarding the source of the picturesque. He maintained, like Burke, that objects themselves had picturesque qualities rather than spectators having picturesque vision. While the outstanding qualities of the sublime had been vastness and obscurity, and those of the beautiful had been smoothness and gentleness, the characteristics of the picturesque were succinctly defined by Price as *"roughness and sudden variation joined to irregularity."*[58]

Irregularity had now become an official principle of the picturesque, and it actually broadened the appreciation for, and the importance of, landscape. Knight, rather than emphasizing in his *Inquiry* views seen from indoors, resolved that "few persons ever look for compositions when within doors. It is in walks or rides through parks, gardens or pleasure grounds that they are allowed to and become subjects of conversation."[59] In our own discussion of ancient theaters in chapter 2, we saw that doorways led to interiors, for the point of view was from outside. During the Renaissance this changed, and the viewer was inside looking through windows and doorways to the landscape "outdoors." As a result of the picturesque developments we have been discussing, the educated person had learned to travel about outdoors judging actual landscape compositions. The techniques of framing, distancing, and irregularly balancing compositions, learned from painting, had been internalized in the spectator.

Price was the earliest writer to suggest, as an alternative to the symmetrical placement of buildings, the orientation of windows toward site features. While this idea placed emphasis on the view from inside, it also resulted in site changes: it forced the building to accommodate itself to the site resulting in irregular, "picturesque" forms and combinations that would not otherwise have occurred. In addition to the outward views and splendidly odd-shaped rooms that resulted, views toward buildings could now be advantageous from many locations. Here we find that the picturesque has led us away from a frontal, singular, one-point-perspective view. The landscape garden perfectly accommodated this situation. Indeed, it was intended to provide a picture from many points of view.

To appreciate the revolutionary character of this move away from symmetry, "it must be remembered that no important building had been completed since the time of Queen Elizabeth that was not symmetrical in itself and that no architect had imagined a serious design in which one-half did not reflect the other."[60] Indeed, buildings were following the lead of the landscape garden, which had itself already broken away from symmetry.

It is not surprising, then, that design on a larger scale, such as town and village planning, is closely connected with the picturesque. When the landscape is the scale of judgment, as was true of the landscape paintings, the context, and thus the composition, is larger than the individual building. Once architects got into the habit of regarding their designs from a distance, and as a part of a larger composition, the idea was accepted that the landscape context should guide the design of buildings.

Price advised those who were rebuilding a village to consider it in relation to the landscape generally, and to that end to study Titian's method of grouping humble houses and villages in an attractive manner. Symmetry and linear development were to be avoided. Inequality of ground, existing trees and bushes, and old buildings were not only to be retained but were to suggest the character of the new buildings.[61] (Blaise Hamlet near Bath, designed at the beginning of the nineteenth century, is a good example of the picturesque village and cottage.)

We can now see how irregularity, a characteristic of the picturesque, had an influence that extended far beyond the narrow confines of gardens. It admitted landscape. The widening of the scale of composition from gardens and buildings to the entire landscape had revised the most basic tenets of design. In fact, the nineteenth-century term *landscape architecture* defines itself—on the basis of this widened scale of composition—as design that recognizes and accommodates an existing context. But the picturesque had still more far-reaching effects, which landscape architecture has yet to fully integrate into its understanding of itself.

Both Price and Knight hoped that designers would get away from the idea of re-creating objects, either in pictures or in landscape, and would instead learn to love color, light, shade, and intricacy *independently of the objects that produced them.*[62] This hope represents the first step away from the progression toward realistic depiction of landscape which we have been observing for five hundred years. If the objects themselves were not the source of picturesque qualities, then there would be no reason to produce increasingly realistic images of them, and as Price suggested, the viewer must be an important part of the equation.

Consequently, by the end of the eighteenth century the picturesque was understood as a mode of vision whose most salient feature is the replacement of symmetry with irregularity. But the picturesque represents much more than the break with symmetry. The kind of individual interpretation recommended by Price meant that all previous standards of beauty were open to question. The separation of content from visual qualities meant that anything—from the ordinary to the violent—could be explored for its potential beauty.

It is easy to guess, particularly from Price's description of "abstract vision," that picturesque vision would result in the impressionism of the late nineteenth century. In the twentieth century, even the total absence of recognizable form would become an end in itself. Without naturalism to convey meanings based on literature once shared, one must instead judge a work of art in relation to its place in the history of seeing.

———

In an important sense, the landscape of eighteenth-century England bears witness to a transformation in the concept of nature. Early in that century the garden still looked orderly and defensive, but as the garden took on all of the painterly attributes discussed since the seventeenth century—irregularity, variety, and distance—"nature" came to mean an irregularly curving clump of trees and a meadow. No longer omnipotent or fearsome, nature became a rural pastoral enclave. Since the garden recognized and incorporated the landscape that lay outside its border, nature, once thought of as beyond the boundaries of the garden, traded places with, indeed became, the garden. Even if it created the illusion of being something greater, the English landscape garden was framed and objectified in much the same way as the geometric gardens that preceded it.

In a corresponding fashion, the landscape was treated more as the garden always had been—as an object of beauty. Both rural landscapes and even (usually from a greater distance) urban ones were judged by the visual criteria used to evaluate paintings and gardens. Although the landscape became recognized for the fact that it was designed, it became an aesthetic object. A comprehensive set of expectations therefore developed: nature should be scenic. It is this same set of expectations, based on painting, which we still depend upon today when, for example, visual resource managers assess federal lands on the basis of form, line, color, and texture, independently of content.[63]

Nature, at least as it was represented by the forms of England's landscape garden, was an object conceived by eighteenth-century aristocrats. Seeing the garden, nature, and the landscape change in form and meaning, we have learned that many of the qualities we think of as inherent are really culturally constructed. As a result, we have taken a great step toward naming our own subjectivity. We have begun to see the landscape more as a reflection of ourselves.

Pictorialization Naturalized   III

10

Democratic Landscape: Nineteenth-Century America

> Beginning in the 1820's and continuing through the next de-
> cades, artists and writers began to proclaim their need to be out
> in the fields or on the rivers, sketching trees and flowers in God's
> quiet landscape, far from the evil haunts of man. . . . The natural
> result of such an exodus was a decline in portraiture, a social
> art, and an increase in the solitary act of landscape painting.[1]

From this short statement, we learn much about nineteenth-century
American attitudes. The landscape had become a repository of goodness, linked with God's name. This is a stunning reversal of the guilt
Petrarch felt for looking at an earthly prospect: now the earth is a
manifestation of God. In contrast to the evils of society, the rural
landscape was deemed worthy of devotion, for in the countryside solitary activities, such as observing and sketching, could be pursued.
Clearly, such an attitude is reminiscent of Tityrus's pastoral setting,
which was both far from Rome and secure from the threats of nature.

In the nineteenth century, the Virgilian pastoral concept traveled
to America, not only to reappear in painting and design but also to
be posited in the landscape itself. The classic shepherd's motive—to
withdraw from the world and begin a new life in a fresh, green landscape—seemed destined for the New World.[2] But there is a crucial
difference: while the pastoral had been an illusion in Virgil's poetry
and Claude's painting, and only a re-creation of an illusion in an
early landscape garden like Stowe, the American continent, seen by
its European-derived settlers as practically devoid of a past, provided
an actual landscape upon which to implement the ancient pastoral
concept. Furthermore, it was just at this time that the profession of
landscape architecture and, not coincidentally, the world's first public
parks came into existence.

It was precisely at this moment of transition from the illusionistic
mode to the actual American landscape that sentimental pastoralism
gained strength. As Leo Marx puts it: "What is attractive in pastoralism is the felicity represented by an image of a natural landscape,
either unspoiled or, if cultivated, rural. Movement toward such a
symbolic landscape also may be understood as movement away from
an 'artificial' world, a world identified with 'art,' using this word in

its broadest sense to mean the disciplined habits of mind or arts developed by organized communities. In other words, this impulse gives rise to a symbolic motion away from centers of civilization toward their opposite, nature, away from sophistication toward simplicity, or, to introduce the cardinal metaphor of the literary mode, away from the city toward the country. When this wish is unchecked, the result is a simple-minded wishfulness, a romantic perversion of thought and feeling."[3] To put this same point in terms of Virgil's poetry, the rise in sentimental pastoralism meant that Meliboeus and everything he represents was forgotten.

"Sentimental pastoralism" is an accurate description of America's most popular landscape paintings in the nineteenth century. Owing much to the compositional conventions of Claude and the Dutch of the seventeenth century, and reinforced by the theory of the picturesque of the following century, the nineteenth century produced the greatest profusion of landscape painting in the history of art. Despite the fact that the landscape faced extensive destruction in a fast-paced, growing consumer economy, nothing negative, either natural or cultural was depicted in these paintings.

The undeveloped landscape of the United States made it vulnerable to many associations. "Landscape could eventually become the proper American religious art, suitable to the idea that God had given this land to this nation, and then come to dwell in it as the local abiding Soul of Nature—a pure spirit, democratic and non-denominational."[4] Observing a vaguely defined, contradictory "nature" practically became a national obsession. But what was this nature? Essentially it was defined negatively: it was conceived as the absence of people and the absence of natural threats.

The near absence of either a written cultural history or built culture in the form of great cities in America meant that the continent could not compete with Europe's cultural antiquity. New discoveries in geology, however, supported the idea that geological time was vastly longer than historical time. Claude's worn, rocky outcrops, for example, were abundant in the American landscape and could be seen as far more ancient than even Greek ruins. From this point of view, the "nature" of the New World could be seen as superior to the "culture" represented by the Old.

Barbara Novak, in *Nature and Culture*, claims that Americans' thoughts about nature manifested themselves most clearly in two distinct types of landscape painting: popular and luminist. The former were large-scale, operatic paintings by such artists as Frederic Church, Albert Bierstadt, and Thomas Moran, and included the paintings of the Hudson River School as well as paintings of the West. These works followed European conventions and reinforced the myth of a bigger, more progressive, yet older America. The luminists also recognized earlier compositional conventions, though they succeeded in transcending them. Together, the reflective qualities of the luminist paintings and the notions of progress depicted in the popular paintings will tell us much about nineteenth-century American attitudes toward the landscape.

Both forms of painting reinforced the notion of America as a land protected from civilization, yet both depended on highly civilized artistic conventions. Although one might assume that the very different-looking landscape of the New World would necessarily result in very different-looking paintings, the dependence on European painting conventions proved otherwise. Even with all the emphasis on the documentation of actual places in America, artists' compositions and choice of views were influenced more by European conventions of landscape painting than by their own landscape. Again, cultural conventions for illuminating nature were critical in establishing the way we see. The very notion of a "new world" obviously presupposed the presence of an "old world." This old world did the defining, and provided a way of seeing which was then superimposed on the vast terrain of the United States.

Popular Pictures

Once the American landscape had become a repository of national pride, cultivating its appreciation became one of the key preoccupations of the age. Of course, landscapes were not appreciated equally; none rated higher than the rural and the seemingly wild. In 1855, Ashur B. Durand, a pioneer with Thomas Cole in the Hudson River School, called forthrightly for a wilderness art. "'Go not abroad then in search of material for the exercise of your pencil,' he wrote in the *Crayon*, 'while the virgin charms of our native land have claims on your deepest affections.' America's 'untrodden wilds,' Durand continued, 'yet spared from the pollutions of civilization, afford a guarantee for a reputation of originality that you may elsewhere long seek and find not.'"[5] Ironically, it was Durand who in a painting entitled *Progress* (fig. 10.1) depicted the coming of civilization to the wilderness, and did so almost entirely in terms borrowed from Claude.

This large (four-by-six-foot) painting is practically divided in half. "On the left of that picture are vestiges of the picturesque—a storm, a ravaged tree, and even Indians, emblems of the 'old nature.' New nature, at the right, is the Garden in which the puffs of smoke from steamboats, buildings, and a locomotive inoffensively announce the age of progress."[6] Apparently, it is a blessing if progress eventually usurps the wilderness. Durand does not picture the costs of this progress; even the ravaged trees in the foreground show us that their destruction was not by the tools of civilization but by the innocence of nature.

Fig. 10.1. Asher B. Durand, *Progress* (1853). The Warner Collection of Gulf States Paper Corporation, Tuscaloosa, Alabama.

Behind the broken stumps are the upright, high-branching, lacy trees familiar from Claude's paintings. A small coulisse is formed where three Indians look out toward the billows of smoke that symbolize American progress. The picture is composed diagonally, with the primary diagonal formed by the outline of the foreground vegetation against the river and the sky. This device was frequently used by Claude; it leads the eye to the distance, dividing foreground from middle ground and, in this case, progress from the past.

The near absence of figures in an American landscape painting is loaded with meaning. The spectator, with no surrogate to license entry into the picture, is all eyes; and the open space suggests that looking is a spiritual act of wonder and purification. Novak suggests that one type of figure can be introduced into this landscape without disrupting this relationship between the spectator and the view: the Indian. A function of "nature," the Indian could symbolize the land's unexplored state. Like the forests, the Indian exists in a state of nature, immune from the ravages of Western culture; at least before he too is cut down.[7]

Novak suggests that in American landscape painting a progression could be observed similar to one that had earlier been followed in European painting. In the American progression, the linear mode could be exemplified by early topographic recordings; it was followed by the painterly mode, as exemplified by the lively rock masses in Moran's *Grand Canyon* or Bierstadt's *The Rocky Mountains, Lander's Peak* (fig. 10.3). Novak takes this idea a step further by suggesting that even the perception of the new landscape was interrupted by these pictorial conventions. "This suggests that the process of discovery itself, as it developed its own history and past, became subject to the 'civilizing,' along with the verbal associations, withdrew newness from the terrain at the very moment it was exalting it. The act of seeing was a form of possession that donated to the new landscape those perceptual habits we call conventions, in turn determined by the ideas of the age."[8] Therefore, the assumption that the experience of a new landscape would naturally produce new pictorial conventions requires amending. Americans awestruck before these painted natural wonders were often viewing them through European spectacles, literally and figuratively. They were using the "Claude glasses" of the seventeenth century, and their very point of view was inherited from Europe.

Elevation and grandeur were depicted by American artists according to the European formula for "ideal" landscapes. Claude's pastoral compositions had such an impact on late eighteenth-century European art that American artists seemed to believe that only by adopting Claude's conventions could they ensure their work's acceptance in the art world. These conventions assured American painters that they were "framing" the landscape artfully, thus making "art out of nature." The adoption of Claude's compositional techniques became so widespread that his landscape formulas soon became virtual clichés in American art.

Why did Claudian conventions persist so tenaciously even when American artists wanted to invent their own distinctive art, become sensitive to their own locale, and identify with their own form of government? What Novak has to say in response to this question could as easily explain why landscape architects have held so tenaciously to the forms of the English landscape garden that were derived from the same painting conventions: "*They annexed a museum culture they could only experience as visitors.* Thus the Claudian mode remained a vital force in America long after the so-called classical tradition in European landscape had been modified. Also, the pastoral aspect of the Claudian convention reinforced those myths of America as a new Eden that were so important in the nineteenth century."[9]

In annexing a "museum culture," Americans were able to revisit the greatest moment in landscape painting and transport its conventions to their own landscape. By adopting Claude, they also adopted Virgil and the pictorial conventions that had grown in Italy before the Industrial Revolution. Landscape painters illustrated American progress with the old aristocratic and pastoral conventions. With this apparently contradictory approach, they could both take advantage of the newness of their own land and yet produce stable and reassuring images of it that would deny that the American landscape was undergoing rapid change.

Luminism

The luminists produced works whose attitude and form was different than those of the popular landscape paintings. According to Novak, they were "classic rather than baroque, contained rather than expansive, aristocratic rather than democratic, private not public, introverted not gregarious, exploring a state of being rather than becoming."[10] She has characterized the "operatically sublime" popular paintings as using every last ounce of convention in pursuit of attention. By contrast, the quietistic and apparently modest paintings now called luminist recognize convention while redefining it, and find their prototypes not in Claude but in the Dutch tradition. This latter fact is, perhaps, not surprising, since the Dutch republic of the seventeenth century—with its Protestantism, its respect for humble things, and its middle-class citizens—shares basic affinities with America of the nineteenth century.

In a luminist painting, monumentality seems to be accomplished through scale rather than size. A perfect, miniaturized universe offers the spectator an irresistible invitation to empathize. The spectator is urged to conceptualize scale and enter the luminist arena in which figures, when they exist at all, are no larger than twigs. These luminist paintings were not as widely liked as the "popular" paintings, but they had a small and devoted audience. "It is very possible that the artists distinguished between a public and a private role to which appropriate conventions might be assigned, and that there existed a public and a private taste."[11]

The general public, for example, had a great need for convention. Even if they were not knowledgeable about the seventeenth-century conventions that informed the popular and highly anthropocentric landscape paintings, they felt these paintings' familiarity. By contrast, the transcendental luminists sought to lose sight of themselves in the midst of spiritual experience. In their quiet tranquility, luminist paintings express a new concept of sublimity, and the infusion of the divine is no longer entirely mediated by the theatrical trappings of Italian conventions.

In *Lake George*, a painting by John Frederick Kensett, the landscape is transparent to the power of light (fig. 10.2). The visual corollary of silence is stillness. Stillness and silence are opposites of the noise and action we saw in Durand's painting *Progress* (fig. 10.1). Yet the private quietude of the luminists was ignored by the public in

Fig. 10.2. John Frederick Kensett, *Lake George* (1869). Bequest of Maria DeWitt Jesup, 1915 (15.30.61), Metropolitan Museum of Art, New York.

favor of the more active popular paintings, which often, like the works of Church and Bierstadt, invited easy entry by their very size. Independence from Claudian conventions and recourse to Dutch examples required unframed vistas and the attempt to make the spectator an inhabitant of the landscape rather than an elevated onlooker. Infinity, endless vistas, and quiet assist solitary contemplation. Horizontal space allows for a different kind of prospect than does the vista framed by trees.

To move from Claude's landscape conventions to those of the Dutch or the luminists is thus to relocate oneself geographically. It is like moving from the northeastern or northwestern United States to the Great Plains or an ocean island. Claude's conventions were inspired by partially forested, partially cultivated sites in Italy. They were translated into design in heavily forested England. But the Dutch paintings were inspired in a flooded landscape, the vista wide open and deeply panoramic.

Luminism contributed little to the myth of the expanding frontier. As a result, the preponderance of luminist paintings were of the East rather than the American West. Still, it is to the West that we must now move, to a landscape of monumentally sized mountains where we shall find something of immense importance to America's conception of itself: an image of wilderness.

The celebration of landscape and the obsession with "nature" in nineteenth-century America coincided, rather ironically, with the relentless destruction of the land. Idealized and nationalistic attitudes expressed in landscape paintings, however, were finally useful in establishing a greater appreciation for spectacular wild places, for these paintings helped to create an attitude favorable to the establishment of the world's first publicly preserved enclaves of wilderness, the national parks. Even Yellowstone National Park is affiliated with, and its protection is even a consequence of, scenic habits cultivated by centuries of landscape painting.

As mentioned several times already, the appreciation of rural and wild landscapes originates in the cities. In the nineteenth century, once again, the beginnings of wilderness appreciation were found among writers, artists, scientists, and vacationers—people, in short, who did not live in rural areas or face wilderness from the pioneer's perspective. Early American pioneers rightfully feared and were hostile toward the wilderness; after all, it immediately threatened their survival. Only when the colonists had cleared trees and made the landscape suit their needs could they look appreciatively at the forest that remained. The artist's job was to keep ahead of the axe and illustrate this newly discovered appreciation. Ironically, although city-dwellers admired America's wilderness and were also advocates for its preservation, cities themselves were regarded with a hostility once reserved for wild forests. The American conception of wilderness which produced our national parks is thus very similar to Tityrus's conception of the pastoral: a comfortable enclave without threat from either the city or cruel nature.

George Catlin, an early painter of the American landscape, was the first to move beyond regret about the loss of wilderness and to envision its preservation. Catlin was convinced that the "primitive" was worthy of our protection because "the further we become separated from that pristine wildness and beauty, the more pleasure does the mind of enlightened man feel in recurring to those scenes." Others said as much, but Catlin's 1832 reflections went further in promoting the idea that Indians, buffalo, and the wilderness in which they existed might not have to yield completely to civilization if the government would protect them in "*a magnificent park* . . . a beautiful and thrilling specimen for America to preserve and hold up to the view of her refined citizens and the world, in future ages! A *nation's Park*, containing man and beast, in all the wild[ness] and freshness of their nature's beauty!"[12]

Albert Bierstadt, one of America's most popular wilderness painters, included in his scenes all the ingredients Catlin wished to protect: Indians, buffalo, and mountain wilderness. His six-by-ten-foot painting *The Rocky Mountains, Lander's Peak* (fig. 10.3), documented and glorified spectacular mountain views. His work not only captured the American imagination but actually assisted in the campaign for the establishment of the first national parks late in the nineteenth century. Bierstadt's paintings emphasize prospect—the overwhelming greatness of the American West.

The cloud-capped mountains and sparkling lakes in Bierstadt's works owe much of their magic to their Dutch pictorial heritage. A painting such as *The Rocky Mountains, Lander's Peak* looks accessible not so much to exploration or to tourism, but to vision itself. Furthermore, Bierstadt also exploited the new technology that painters had resorted to throughout the nineteenth century, namely the camera. The camera had been established as the prime purveyor of visual fact by the middle of the century, and artists had depended upon photographs just as they had always used sketches. But this is not to imply that a painting like *The Rocky Mountains, Lander's Peak* is a documentary picture of the actual place. In *Moving Pictures*, Anne Hollander makes it clear that Bierstadt took many liberties with the facts: "Bierstadt's staggering vistas were cooked up later in the studio, out of sketches and partial camera views, and it would be correct to say that later photography of the West, especially the inviting kind that found its way onto the great blow-ups in Grand Central Station or onto countless calendars, and then into the cinematography of countless Westerns, owes its origins to the inventions of Bierstadt, who showed what it ought to do."[13]

Bierstadt's juxtapositions of disparate views are seamless; the authenticity of his place-making is convincing. Yet reflecting on the actual landscapes, we realize to what extent he has made an awe-inspiring mythology out of the American wilderness. Likewise, the spectacular images of scenery we know so well in movies—mountains at sunset, or a waterfall at dawn—provoke their spectators both to gasp and to think of their own insignificance, and then to make self-congratulatory claims for dominion over these wonders.

In the nineteenth-century paintings we have seen, both Italian and Dutch pictorial conventions have been incorporated into the American view of recognizable places, such as *The Rocky Mountains, Lander's Peak*. These paintings follow no narrative; they simply pictorialize the American landscape. In that sense, they are documentary. But even in the process of documenting a place, they give us the illusion of seeing it. The window remains in place, perpetuating the illusion. However, when we compare Bierstadt's painting to a photograph of Lander's Peak (e.g., fig. 10.4), we have some sense of the grandeur Bierstadt contrived. Such a comparison, however, should not suggest that the photo itself is the authentic truth. It, too, is a picture and must be experienced quite differently than the actual place.

Fig. 10.3. Albert Bierstadt, *The Rocky Mountains, Lander's Peak* (1863). Rogers Fund, 1907 (07.123), Metropolitan Museum of Art, New York.

Fig. 10.4. Lander's Peak, 1987. Photograph by Jeff Jacobson.

Pictures like Bierstadt's and the photograph of Lander's Peak are so powerful that the actual experience of being in places such as the Rocky Mountains may be colored by having seen the pictorial rendering. But we must remember that the pictorial experience itself, and the experience motivated by pictures, is much like Tityrus's experience in the pasture as hymned by Virgil. Even though America's first national parks, the world's first wilderness areas protected by a government, were not wholly designed places, they, as well as the paintings such as Bierstadt's that led to their preservation, were very much inspired by the pastoral ideal. They are framed enclaves of an ideal wilderness whose spectators are protected and comfortable.

The Railroad Intrudes into the Pastoral

There is one powerful industrial force that made its way into the American wilderness unprotested: the railroad. Its depiction in the painted wilderness of the nineteenth century, however, deserves special consideration, because the train entered this medium only with difficulty. First, it had to be disguised as a delicate puff of smoke. Only later, as we shall see, did it appear as an intruder. Such an intrusion, I propose, parallels the presence of Meliboeus in the pastoral scene Virgil created in the first book of the *Eclogues*. Like the train, Meliboeus represents the alien world encroaching from without, the world of great cities such as Rome and, along with it, organized power and authority. The train also stands for a more sophisticated, complex style of life than the one represented by rural simplicity. Its central function is to expose the concept of the pastoral (and that of the wilderness) to the pressure of change—to an encroaching world of power and complexity.

The trains that discretely populate the American landscape paintings of the mid-century are remote and insignificant. The symbol of the new age of steam is represented as a distant twist of smoke, beneath which the eye searches for the linked line that indicates the presence of the new invention. Repeatedly, one's eyes detect a train in landscape paintings where its presence had not before been perceptible. For a good example, look back again at Durand's *Progress* (fig. 10.1) and find the train in the "new nature" to the right.

Artists were reluctant to depict the train in all its mechanical fury. We can easily imagine, for example, buffalo taking the place of Tityrus's sheep in paintings of the West, but it is much more difficult to imagine industrial machinery conforming to the pastoral ideal. This resistance to change is quite similar to that felt by today's designers. Again and again, we find that design aims to screen and disguise, rather than honestly confront, today's technological intrusions (e.g., cars and satellite dishes) in twentieth-century pastoral creations.

"In art, we have a fascinating history of technological inventions presenting art conventions with no option but to exclude them. The automobile in twentieth-century art provided one such example. There were few effective ways of including it within an existing realistic convention until the appearance of American pop art."[14] Likewise, landscape architects have been screening cars in parking lots with vegetation and walls for decades in a similar attempt to disguise the pervasive presence of the car, and therefore technology, in their pastoral designs. (SITE, Inc., broke away from this convention in 1977 when it lined up a row of cars at the entrance of a shopping mall parking lot in Hamden, Connecticut, and camouflaged them with a cover of the parking lot's asphalt, literally hiding the cars and at the same time turning them into a visual screen.)

To truthfully depict the intrusion of the railroad into a scenic landscape painting, one replete with pastoral and aristocratic connotations, was equally difficult. The compositional conventions learned from Claude and Rosa would not gracefully allow it. According to Novak, "in American prints—the popular form of the nineteenth century—contemporary with the paintings, the train receives full foreground examination. The prints were a form of reportage: this is how the beast looked."[15] Novak's example is a Currier and Ives picture (fig. 10.5). Instead of trying to make "nature" into art, these popular prints were a form of reportage that did not try to screen the present from view. Even though the print's aerial point of view disguises the picture somewhat, the train's bulky presence and the sense of power are conveyed even as the train crosses the picture plane, smoking and lurching.

One artist whose career reflects the tension between accurate reportage and a loyalty to the conventions of the pastoral in painting was George Inness. In 1854, he broke with pastoral convention by bringing the train into the foreground and, at the same time, in *The Lackawanna Valley* (fig. 10.6), he managed to paint a scenic picture of the Lackawanna Railroad Company's operations. At the first, apparently, the commission repelled him. Hitherto a painter of pleasant and on the whole conventionally pastoral landscapes, Inness was put off by the notion of painting anything as devoid of visual charm as a repair shop, a roundhouse, or a smoking locomotive. He did not see how such objects could be assimilated into his habitual Virgilian mode. But, as it happens, the difficulty proved to be stimulating, and the result is generally included among his best works.[16]

Cleverly, he has used the train as a unifying device. The hills in the background and the trees of the middle distance envelop the indus-

Fig. 10.5. Currier and Ives (after Frances Flora Palmer), *Across the Continent: Westward the Course of Empire Takes Its Way* (1868). The Thomas Gilcrease Institute of American History and Art, Tulsa, Oklahoma.

Fig. 10.6. George Inness, *The Lackawanna Valley* (1855). Gift of Mrs. Huttleston Rogers, National Gallery of Art, Washington, D.C.

trial buildings and artifacts precisely as Claudian conventions would dictate. No sharp lines set off the built forms from the terrain. Blending, a very familiar concept to environmental designers and closely related to screening, is the key here. The cottony puffs of smoke that rise from the engine and the roundhouse are not unpleasant. They are merely duplicates of those that rise from behind the church—an ingenious touch.

Instead of cutting the space into sharp, rectilinear segments as railroad tracks often do, the right-of-way curves gracefully across the center of the canvas, where it divides in two and forms the delicate ovals that dominate the middle plane. It is noteworthy, too, that the animals in the pasture continue to graze or rest peacefully as the tidy, diminutive train approaches. Still, this is not a lament for cherished land; the stumps are not aged remnants of trees that had fallen in old age or by storm, like those we saw in the foreground of Durand's *Progress*. They have clearly been cut down in their prime; this pasture has been chopped out of a wilderness.

Finally, it is the solitary, reclining figure who establishes the quiet, relaxed mood. He has no sheep, but he contemplates the sight in the serene posture of the good shepherd looking out across Arcadia. Inness has allowed industrial subject matter to intrude upon the pasture, but the spectator, like the shepherd, is still comforted by the pastoral scene we have seen forming for centuries.

Nineteenth-century American landscape painters were quite serious and, for the most part, totally innocent of irony. Novak suspects some irony in Inness's work, however, in his portrayal of the train, which she believes he has glorified, and in the presence of the stumps in the foreground: "Inness's feelings are directly opposed to one of the central concerns of the Hudson River School—the pictorial hymning of America's purity and power through wilderness landscape."[17] Novak concludes that the mysteriousness of this picture may be an assertion of the modernity of Inness's art. We cannot be sure, particularly when our own attitudes toward the train and technology have changed so drastically in this century.

Inness painted *The Lackawanna Valley* within a few years of the first use of the term *landscape architecture*. This small historical coincidence says much: landscape architecture is a profession inextricably linked to compositional conventions that make pastoral and even wilderness landscapes scenic. Yet, as Inness has illustrated, the landscape, even a wholly designed one, must somehow allow contemporary culture to intrude upon its conventions. As *The Lackawanna Valley* shows, acknowledging the less-than-ideal aspects of the present, particularly the technological, is no easy task.

The pastoral ideal has been central to landscape architecture's very definition of itself, and while it supplies the illusion of freedom, its very well established and, at times, intractable conventions tell us how restrictive it really is. It is one of the ironies of the pastoral ideal that even though it reflects a deeply antiurban sentiment, it has always been primarily an urban phenomenon. Henry Thoreau, for example, grew up and was educated in Boston before he became the most eloquent spokesman for an attitude that scorned social relations and idealized solitary contemplation. His acreage at Walden Pond, where the sounds of the train could still be heard, was an American version of the traditional refuge of the city dweller. Just like an elaborate garden located some distance from Rome, Walden Pond was a safe and "wild" landscape not far from Boston.

What landscape could better provide the comforts necessary for solitary and leisurely contemplation than a pastoral one? Designers thus introduced the pastoral vision into cities by locating "rural" cemeteries there, an American landscape invention that occasionally took its cues directly from pictures. Mount Auburn Cemetery (1831) in Cambridge, Massachusetts, for example, was a richly layered environment that retained features of the English landscape garden but was also curiously American. When it was begun, there were probably but a handful of important American landscape paintings of the Hudson River School. However, as the somewhat miniaturized landscape of the cemetery evolved in the 1840s, the canvases of Thomas Cole and Asher B. Durand certainly must have been known to its designers. Specific scenes may even have been called to mind: the castellated tower atop Auburn's Mount is a smaller evocation of Cole's *Valley of Vaucluse* (1841); and the hilly terrain of the site, with its gothic chapel and monuments, recalls Durand's *The Evening of Life* (1840), part of a series of canvases on the cyclical pattern of life and death.[18]

More important than the introduction of cemeteries in cities, however, was the development of the public park. Indeed, there is probably no greater example of the influence of the scenic habits whose history we have been tracing than the idea of constructing urban public parks designed to embody the pastoral ideal in the midst of society. Central Park and all its variations in cities across the United States tried to fulfill the American dream by combining the solitary experience, so prized by the eighteenth and nineteenth centuries, with the aristocratic pictorial conventions inherited from Europe. Frederick Law Olmsted succeeded in doing just that, and remained adamant in his belief that a designed landscape like that of Central Park should maintain the illusion of being rural country.

It is in suburbia, at the boundary between city and country, that

Americans have demonstrated their ceaseless dependence on the pastoral ideal. Here, individuals can purchase their own piece of the pastoral dream without becoming shepherds themselves or abandoning entirely the benefits of the city. The segregation of houses and neighborhoods from one another as well as from areas zoned for the differing land uses disguises conflict. The isolation of dwellings from their neighbors by profuse plantings reflects the belief that one should always strive for freedom from society. Suburbia's strengthened boundaries and pastoral appearance not only help guard the individual's property and privacy but also intentionally withdraw private property from the social and public world.

Despite the variety of designs in which landscape architects were involved in the nineteenth century, and their many fine innovations—cemeteries, city parks, campuses, suburbs, and national parks—all of these designs, despite their differences in size and purpose, can be easily interpreted in terms of Tityrus's pastoral ideal. This is because the most significant relationship is not between people but between the design itself and the terrain. Contoured streets, the ingenious and often sensitive exploitation of every topographical feature, the ubiquitous presence of the curve even when there are no existing features to circumvent—in short, the picturesque irregularity of traditional landscape design—gives ample testimony to a pastoral ideal bereft of Meliboeus.[19]

This tradition, however, could not last forever, and at the very same time that landscape architects were designing naturalistic parks and suburbs, the language of the very landscape painting that had given form to the pastoral ideal was superseded. Toward the end of the nineteenth century the scenic "window" view to the world outside, its attendant painting conventions, and even the very scenic habits on which it was based began to shatter. The window had become a mirror that no longer reflected an accurate image. In fact, the whole comfortable idea of imitating nature, and picturing it as a view framed by trees, was beginning to disintegrate: artists, particularly in France, were exploring and seeing the landscape anew.

Fracturing the Pictorial Conventions of Naturalism

Late in the nineteenth century, French artists broke down the conventions that had been used for centuries, first to create the naturalistic view in paintings and then to reshape the landscape itself. These artists destroyed lines that distinguished objects from one another; abandoned shading that had provided three-dimensional modeling; and broke down the central composition, the static imposition of perspective, and even the idea of pictorial authority. Some of them were given the name "impressionists," derogatorily, because they seemed to believe that a brief impression was worthy of being painted and called "nature."

Edouard Manet and his fellow artists alerted themselves to what they took to be the misconceptions of naturalistic painting as early as the 1860s. They claimed that we do not always see individual objects, each with its own color and even gradation of shade. Instead, objects and shadows have many colors, which blend in our minds. Spectators had learned the conventions of shading so well from pictures that when Manet reminded them, in his paintings, that outside, in the full light of day, some round forms really do look flat, like a patch of color, they were outraged.

It was not only the technique of impressionist painting which so outraged the critics; it was also the choice of subject. Since the sixteenth century, painters had been expected to look for a corner of nature which, through their own re-composition, could come to be seen as picturesque. For example, Claude had portrayed in a picturesque way Roman ruins set in a pastoral landscape (e.g., fig. 8.1). And by the early eighteenth century, "the picturesque" was wholly defined by those very scenes that painters had already composed.

By contrast, impressionist painters abandoned religious and historical subjects composed in pastoral landscapes. Instead, they concentrated on creating immediate and faithful renderings of the actual landscapes that were before their eyes. Claude Monet, for example, found beauty in an industrialized landscape and painted a Paris railway station in *The Gare St-Lazare: Arrival of a Train* (fig. 10.7). This didn't strike the critics as an important subject, and even Monet may not have been so interested in the railway station as a place. But he did see it as an opportunity to illustrate nature. This may sound confusing: how can a railway station illustrate nature? However, the confusion arises only because we have become so accustomed to the idea of the green meadow and the forest as nature. By introducing contemporary subject matter, Monet was making a break with the pastoral conventions that had not allowed the train to enter the scene. Constantly changing effects of light and air interested him. Nature, so defined, could change from minute to minute as the steam of an engine filled the air or the wind scattered a reflection in a lily pond.

Though it is based on acute observation, Monet's style of painting destroys the illusion of looking at the world through a window. We can see the use of thick brush strokes to provide the flickering patches of color that our eyes see when they dart about evaluating the outside world. The technique of using thick, messy strokes eliminates any possibility of interpreting the picture plane as a plane of glass. Instead, the painting immediately proclaims itself to be a representation of a momentary experience of nature, and not a view of nature seen through a window.

Fig. 10.7. Claude Monet, *The Gare St-Lazare: Arrival of a Train* (1877). Bequest–Collection of Maurice Wertheim, Class of 1906, Fogg Art Museum, Harvard University, Cambridge, Massachusetts.

Not all painters of this period considered themselves impressionists. Edgar Degas, for example, thought his paintings too contrived to be considered impressions. "A painting," he said, "is an artificial work existing outside nature and it requires as much cunning as the perpetration of a crime."[20] Nevertheless, Degas experimented with images that at least gave the appearance of being uncomposed. By doing this, he and other artists of the time were calling basic scenic conventions into question. Rather than portraying a centered and balanced view plucked from its surroundings, Degas cut off his main subject—dancers—with the frame. The dancers appear to be "accidentally" off-center, as if we had caught them in a moment they were not posed for, as at a rehearsal. The spectator seems to see a "backstage" interlude, a scene that has not been composed to look like a performance in which the viewer would be central to the stage. The graceful movement of the dancers has been suddenly arrested—by the frame.

In paintings such as those of Monet and Degas, the frame is no longer an object designed to give the canvas the illusion of space; the painting itself is an object. It is a surface rather than a view, a moment rather than a respite. Georges Seurat even painted some of his frames with dots of color, like those in his painting, thereby negating the illusionary device for framing a view. In fact, most contemporary paintings do not have frames at all, because they no longer serve the purpose of creating a window to distant space.

Painters such as Vincent van Gogh also stressed flatness, and even distorted perspective, so as to be more expressive and less factual. In Van Gogh's painting of a wheat field, for example, he emphasized the foreground, which had formerly been empty or had provided refuge to the spectator outside the painting. The field is seen from a knee-level position that obstructs any view of the middle ground or the background or any need for deep perspective. It asks us to bend down to experience a wheat field and, while we are kneeling, it questions our authority.

Paul Cézanne thought very carefully about how his eyes moved about, quickly perceiving color and light. Indeed, it is precisely the process of seeing that becomes the subject of his painting. "No previous painter had taken the viewers through this process so frankly. In Titian or Rubens, it is the final form that matters, the triumphant illusion. . . . The Renaissance admired an artist's certainty about what he saw. But with Cézanne, . . . doubt becomes part of the painting's subject. Indeed, the idea that doubt can be heroic, if it is locked into a structure as grand as that of the paintings of Cézanne's old age, is one of the keys to our century, a touchstone of modernity itself."[21] Such doubt is necessary to question the conventions and explode the scenic habits that had for more than a millennium led to the pictorialization of nature.

Whatever the initial resistance to impressionist paintings, people learned to appreciate them once the first shock had worn off. Even further, these spectators went into the fields and woods, or looked out of their windows onto the Paris boulevards, and found to their delight that the visible world could, after all, be seen in terms of these bright patches of color. The impressionists had taught them to see nature anew. The transposition worked, and a new experience of seeing came into being, because spectators had declared their independence from the familiar naturalistic conventions that had formed their scenic habits for centuries. They learned to explore an unexpected nature and to experience the environment in a way that the old paintings simply could not supply.

In an important sense, however, impressionism continues a very old tradition, for once again pictures changed habits of seeing that had been programmed by earlier pictures. Impressionism had furthered the primary goal of the picturesque: namely, to transfer the artist's visual experience to the beholder. It should be clear that the art of the twentieth century, such as cubism or abstract impressionism, required the radical innovations of impressionism. What is perhaps not so clear, and will be the subject of the next chapter, is that this new way of seeing has finally entered into the design of actual landscapes.

———

Nineteenth-century American landscape paintings depicted, and even documented to a certain degree, real landscapes. In fact, documenting the landscape was among their primary roles. They celebrated the new country, invested the landscape with goodness, and idealized the wilderness. Their spectators could look at their own good fortune and congratulate themselves. Naturalistic landscape painting had reached its zenith: not only had the conventions that had been developed to create the illusion of an actual place succeeded, they had indeed portrayed actual landscapes.

Yet an illusion remained: the idea that documentary paintings (or photographs) can represent the landscape objectively. Far from being objective, these pictures reflected a pastoral ideal that had been composed to provide refuge from conflict. Its conventions were so powerful that the intrusion of the train into the pastoral had, at first, to be denied. Later, when its presence could no longer be denied, the train could still be disguised.

At about the time some painters were adjusting their thoughts and their pastoral compositional conventions to recognize industry and cities, the profession of landscape architecture was born. Olmsted's pastoral design for Central Park depended on the illusion of refuge from conflict. The park pretended to be rural country, even though it had been a swamp and was located in the middle of the city.

During its existence, the profession of landscape architecture has shown the same kind of ambivalence toward technology that George Inness illustrated. One of the aspirations of the profession, however, is to design contextually, to be sensitive to landscape in all its deviations. And yet, images of the pastoral ideal have been so deeply etched in our minds through literature and, more graphically, through painting, that the desire to create landscapes that are havens from reality is in continual conflict with the goal of contextual design.

Near the end of the century, in France, the comfortable idea of an idyllic pastoral that excluded the threatening aspects of nature and contemporary culture was shattered by the impressionists. They broke the naturalistic window. The consequences their revolution had for the landscape are still being felt today, and will be explored in the next chapter.

11

The Spectator's Perception: The Twentieth Century

Since the Middle Ages, artists have applied their skill to produce convincing views of the landscape. From the Renaissance to the verge of the twentieth century, great artists had made one discovery after another which allowed them to conjure up an ever more believable picture of the visible world. This centuries-old habit of seeing the outer world in terms of a distant and framed view had become firmly ingrained and, although its progression had not been so utterly linear, landscape painting reached its naturalistic peak by the middle of the nineteenth century.

The painterly conventions used to create this supposed realism eventually exhausted themselves. Not only had the explosion of photography rendered them otiose, but by the late nineteenth century painters themselves began to call them into question. If American painting of the nineteenth century invoked a sentimentalized, pastoral view of the landscape, then the late nineteenth-century French painters might be thought of as a rejuvenated Meliboeus who appeared on the scene to reveal the inadequacy of the Arcadian fantasy.

Quite simply, modern artists no longer produce illusions that attempt to convince us they are natural views. Instead, they demand that traditional pictorial conventions be measured against the actual experiences of the landscape. The focus of modern paintings is blurred, their aim has turned 180 degrees, their subject has changed: it is no longer the view "out there"; instead, it is the perceptual experience of the spectators themselves. The emphasis is on seeing rather than on what is seen.

Many credit Georges Braque and Pablo Picasso with finally shattering the window of static, naturalistic views. These cubists tried to account for how our bodies perceive space—not the distant space that we see through picture planes or windows, but the space our bodies move through each moment. Cubism breaks with Renaissance perspective by looking from many points of view simultaneously, with none having exclusive authority. The piled and rotated, advancing and receding planes of cubism, hovering in space, are in fundamental contrast to the lines of perspective which converge to a single focal point. Cubism denies the singular location of the viewer and, therefore, the frontal view.

These hovering planes are not shocking to us today, for we have had the advantage of many intervening decades to adjust our expectations to them. In fact, we no longer even have to go to the art museum to see them; they are expressed in the buildings and media, in the basic design, of our everyday environment. To document this, one need only consider the fast-moving sequence of images that constitutes a typical television advertisement. It is clear that one must grasp the spirit animating twentieth-century painting in order to understand contemporary design. An unprecedented many-sidedness, rather than a singular and frontal view, defines modern design, and this conception of space can be traced directly back to changes that occurred in painting.[1]

In the wake of cubism, landscape painting became even less naturalistic. In the second decade of the twentieth century, the transcendentalism of some nineteenth-century American landscape painting was distilled into an abstract representation of thought rather than a pictorial representation of a view. Georgia O'Keeffe's painting *Light Coming on the Plains III* (fig. 11.1) is a conception of space itself, pressing against the frame of the picture. "O'Keeffe had intense feelings about nature, especially the open skies and spaces of the plains, and she found in natural configurations, large and small, homologies for the felt experience of the body."[2] This luminous, unbounded space, barely recognizable as landscape, is, expressively at least, a womb. O'Keeffe has succeeded in picturing open spaces, like those of the plains, in terms of prospect and refuge simultaneously.

O'Keeffe's expression of the landscape of the plains is powerful, but the naturalistic conventions that placed the spectator in a particular relationship to a view are gone. Oddly enough, there is a great irony here: many painters, such as Georgia O'Keeffe herself, some impressionists and cubists, and even some later abstract expressionists (at least in their early years), actually painted outdoors and so, unlike Claude, were in a position actually to observe nature. Their observations, however, did not result in naturalistic paintings. This is a powerful reminder of a critical theme of this entire book, namely, that the framed static view seen through the painterly window is not an unambiguous reflection of nature. It is just as likely that O'Keeffe's abstraction of the plains is more evocative of the landscape in which she worked than a naturalistic painting of the same scene could ever be.

The painter who has best expressed the destruction of naturalism is René Magritte, in his painting *The Door to Freedom* (fig. 11.2). The window of Western perspective that has provided us with a distant view of a pastoral scene is depicted in Magritte's painting. The window itself is carefully framed by the stage curtains that first positioned us in front of a scenic landscape two millennia ago. The landscape is seen from the interior point of view we saw develop in Renaissance perspective. A distant clump of trees in a meadow is ir-

Fig. 11.1. Georgia O'Keeffe, *Light Coming on the Plains III* (1917). Amon Carter Museum, Fort Worth, Texas.

regularly placed in such a way that even Capability Brown would approve. We know that it is a landscape: not only has it been framed, it has been modified.

But the window is shattered, and shards of glass have fallen from the frame. Our pictorial skills are so well developed that we can tell very quickly even from the small shards of evidence that the view etched upon them is the very same as the view outside the window.

Fig. 11.2. René Magritte, *The Door to Freedom* (1937). (Copyright 1992 Charly Herscovici/ARS, New York.)

Does Magritte mean to tell us then that the pictorial experience is no different from seeing actual landscapes? Is he telling us that the public still sees, or attempts to see, its landscape in the aristocratic tradition of naturalism, as detached and private spectators?

Or is he reinforcing the idea that neither the view through the window nor the window itself is an actual landscape, that both are pictures? Why would Magritte title an image of broken vision *The Door to Freedom*? Does true freedom require shattering the window of the past, ridding ourselves of the conventions of naturalistic painting? Is Magritte telling us that he knows we have designed landscapes to look like paintings? These questions are not for Magritte to answer; they are questions we must ask of ourselves. The brief survey presented above of the conventions of naturalistic painting was meant to encourage scrutiny of their influence. Only by being fully knowledgeable about such conventions can we—as landscape architects or even as spectators—experience the landscape without being tyrannized by them.

Naturalistic Conventions
Translated into Actual Landscapes

To understand further and document for the final time the power pictorial conventions have had over the development of landscape, we must look for the presence of these conventions in our everyday world. Despite the fact that we have seen the gradual erosion of naturalistic landscape painting in the twentieth century, and despite the fact that many contemporary designs in the built world and the media have already taken this erosion into account, it nevertheless remains the case that the pastoral view is alive and well today. This is particularly true in the field of landscape architecture. While painters may have abandoned their naturalist predecessors, an enormous number of actual landscape designs reveal that their designers enthusiastically (even if unknowingly) conceived of the landscape as a framed and distant view. *Undeniably, the landscape itself has become the repository of pictorial conventions and landscape architecture the perpetuator of the painterly vision.*

Consequently, it is to actual landscapes that we shall next turn. We shall discover three important facts about the relationship between pictures and landscape: first, pictures still motivate spectators to look at particular landscapes; second, the familiar compositional conventions of the view are still applied to the design of popular public places; and third, a pictorialized idea of nature is projected on the landscape.

PICTURES MOTIVATE TOURISTS

The twentieth-century landscape enthusiast follows in the footsteps of the painter-explorers who popularized American landscape "scenes" nearly a century earlier. Who is this twentieth-century spectator, the tourist-visitor who goes to public places for what has now become a designed experience? What motivates this modern-day spectator? Pictures, film, and video.

The language of traditional landscape painting, according to John Berger, was developed to speak about the traveler's, as opposed to the peasant's, view of landscape. "The peasant's interest in the *land* expressed through his actions, is incommensurate with scenic landscape. Most, (not all) European landscape painting was addressed to a visitor from the city, later called a tourist; the landscape is *his* view, the splendour of it is *his* reward."[3] Nineteenth-century Americans painted views of actual places in order to document and idealize them. Such paintings were quickly followed by pictures mechanically produced by the camera. Early photographs, for example, supported the campaign for establishing Yellowstone National Park. Pictures still inspire tourists to travel long distances to see those geysers.

Travelers survey rather than inhabit; they look down from prospects rather than up to the sky for a preliminary forecast of nature's next move. Today's traveler is the tourist who has inherited the scenic view. Sightseeing is the new ritual—everyone does it. Growing up seeing pictures of the Acropolis, the Statue of Liberty, and the Grand Canyon radically affects our own response to places when we actually see them. We become consumers of landscape, seeing what we expect to see. Our expectations are based on images we have seen; our responses are equally complacent. Pictures can make a direct response to something we have not actually seen before exceedingly difficult; and things not previously seen in pictures can easily go unnoticed. Either way, our experience of landscape is overwhelmed by pictures. Even the landscape paintings we have surveyed, once housed in private collections, have themselves become public attractions; they now reside in museums. Giant exhibitions draw massive crowds and are advertised by pictures of pictures.

Children learn at an early age how to "view" landscapes. During drives in the country, adults point out to them noteworthy sights: "Look at the blue mountains in the distance." As adults, will these same children organize such scenes in the viewfinders of their video cameras?

Environmental designers participate in tourism not only as tourists but also as students and professionals. As part of their training, they become overly familiar with the reproduction of sites as images because they are continually shown pictures of places they have never actually seen. Pictures of the Piazza San Marco and the Villa Lante

prompt twentieth-century versions of the Grand Tour. Even more importantly, professionals know that projects designed to look good in
pictures win awards. Designed places have themselves become souvenirs; they remind us of pictures we have seen.

Because of both their training and their tourism, present-day designers often take their favorite historical forms or current cultural
forms from an international index and use them in their own designs.
Images from Renaissance paintings or exotic foreign places, images
of African masks, and Japanese architecture have been torn from
their social and historical context and are available through the media. Content is transported, detached, skewed, and often lost. Buildings, signs, entrances, gardens, graphic logos, interiors, furniture,
and public spaces take lasting images from the past to make fleeting
images today. We quickly learn to doubt the authenticity of what
we see.

PICTORIAL CONVENTIONS INSPIRE
THE DESIGN OF POPULAR PLACES

In our survey of landscape painting, we have learned how paintings
have used particular compositional conventions to confer status upon
the spectator and the sight. Daily we face examples of attempts to
reproduce these pictorial compositions in designs that frame, unify,
center, elevate, and distance some of our most familiar landscapes.
These conventions transform sites into *attractions*. For example, the
very first step in designing scenic attractions[4] is to fortify boundaries
in order to separate such sights from their surroundings and thereby
draw attention to them. This separation was begun as early as Tityrus's pasture: his pastoral domain was severed from both nature and
society. In a similar fashion, the English landscape garden separated
itself from its agricultural surroundings. We might recall that even
paintings were sequestered from the adjacent walls when picture
frames came into use in the fifteenth century. In each case, the perception of context is discouraged.

Today designers frame actual sites by using fencing, planting, gates,
and entrance signs to strengthen boundaries and separate a site from
its surroundings. Consider, for example, how often site plans depict
the encircling belt of trees popularized by Capability Brown. This
idea of strengthening boundaries around sites has become so automatic that "landscaping," in city-planning parlance, has come to
mean decorating the narrow strips of land between the curb and the
parking lot. Regulations now demand "buffer zones" to separate different uses and unsightly objects. Grass, shrubs, and trees are planted
with the intention of hiding the parking lots that lie behind them. We
know that unsightly objects are there because these plantings have
become well-understood signs that what is behind them is in conflict

with the pastoral ideal. Framing is usually an attempt to create an illusion, and today's designs are no exception. Today framing conceals environmental and social conflicts even as it did in Virgil's time.

Advanced framing, or distancing, occurs when the surroundings are forced back from the sight and the space in between is "landscaped." Using this technique, the attraction is "staged." Sixteenth- and seventeenth-century paintings succeeded in distancing spectators from deep horizons—they portrayed prospects. We have learned that distance is necessary for scenic views. On the grandest scale, Versailles and the Washington Monument are framed in this way; so too are corporate headquarters and houses that are set deeply back from the street. Visitors immediately know that the "space between" is directly proportional to the status this device confers upon the site. New suburban houses sit back from the street to gain status at the expense of social isolation.

Elevation is another critical convention transferred from painting to site design. Claude Lorrain perfected the amphitheatrical position for elevating the spectator of his paintings. Today we are familiar with scenic lookouts, identified by signs on the highway; these lookouts are elevated viewing locations that tell spectators, in case they are unaware, that they are looking at a scenic view. Elevating an attraction may also mean literally raising it up to separate it from its surroundings as if it were put on a pedestal, or on a topographic peak. Memorials have always followed this convention of elevating the name, the site, the building, or the figure. That the Vietnam War Memorial, in Washington, D.C., broke with this convention surely sparked the controversy surrounding its approval.

Each of these pictorial conventions can be an effective design tool for the landscape architect. They can be employed straightforwardly to create a traditional view; they can create a flattering pictorial design just to make an ironic point about the power of pictures in our perception of landscape; or, as in the case of Maya Lin's now famous Vietnam War Memorial, they can be rejected altogether to make the point that a tradition has been broken. In any case, it is knowledge of the history of these conventions and the images from which they have developed, and which they have in turn generated, that is needed in order to avoid the most basic mistake inherent in landscape architecture: believing that the framed, distant, perspectival view is somehow a "natural" way of designing.

NATURE IN PICTORIAL DISGUISE

Along with the pictorial conventions that have been translated into the design of our everyday environments has come a pictorialized view of nature. Such a view interprets nature as separate from people, distanced from them as a painting is distanced from its spectators. In this view, nature is spectacularly good looking and a pleasure to visit. But this view is based on a very particular image of nature, most like that found in nineteenth-century American paintings. Before then the cultural narration that had typically informed landscape painting was overt. The decisive move made in the nineteenth century, and the one that was to impact on twentieth-century landscape architecture, was to pretend that culture could be forgotten and indeed was absent altogether.

Today, nature is popularly associated with a particular type of image, the "pasture" with trees which we are accustomed to seeing pictured. Desperately, with the best of intentions but finally hopelessly, landscape architects wish to restore nature to this "natural" state. We seem to believe that such gestures are evidence of stewardship and, most of all, that we are helping to restore nature to that pretty appearance she had before man came along.

We are confused. Tityrus's pasture is not, and never was, nature. It is a powerful literary illusion. The eighteenth-century landscape garden was a shockingly new environmental art form. But today, when the pastoral ideal is casually constructed in actual places, we deceive ourselves into thinking that our use of pastoral forms is a sign that we are living in tune with nature. The pictorial conception of nature has not helped us to develop environmental sensitivity, nor has it fostered the examination of the historical forms that gave rise to it. Today's spectator depends upon a conception of nature as primarily a pleasing, *painterly* view and, ironically, rejects the idea that this perception is culturally based.

Is naturalistic landscape painting to blame for these developments? I doubt it. In our survey of some two thousand years of landscape painting, we have seen painting develop increasingly convincing illusions. By and large, however, such paintings did not attempt to disguise the fact that they were cultural products. How could they? But nineteenth-century American landscape painters provided images that surely nudged us toward a pictorial conception of nature. Because these painters took a more documentary stance toward their work than landscape painters ever had, their works have often been interpreted as if they had been painted by neutral witnesses observing nature in a (relatively) unmodified state. Their images of trees, mountains, and rivers have been thought to represent nature as it actually was. We know that, in fact, these painters were using European conventions to depict spectacular sights, and they did not picture certain other sights that they also witnessed: unmodified "nature" that was unsightly—swamps and deserts, for example.

From a century of familiarity with their painterly images, we have inherited the idea that nature is spectacular in appearance and separate from culture. But when this attitude toward nature met the railroad on nineteenth-century American canvases, its inherent conflicts surfaced. What was the response? Screen the locomotive from Tity-rus's sight. Pretend that the pasture does not depend on the swamp or the city. Disguise culture. From our survey of landscape painting, we know that the nineteenth-century paintings are exceptions. In fact, from Roman times until well into the Industrial Revolution, cultural modification had been seen as an improvement upon nature.[5] But no longer. Now that we have created havoc with natural systems and daily use tremendous amounts of resources, we confer goodness on whatever we longingly call "natural," and we deem unsightly those very places where we spend most of our days.

The profession of landscape architecture was founded at the same time as the mid-nineteenth-century American paintings were being painted. It is therefore not surprising that the guiding attitudes of these two quintessentially American phenomena are so similar. Indeed, one of landscape architecture's principal (although usually implicit) tenets is that each and every view of the landscape should disguise its dependence on cultural modification, regardless of the extent of that dependence. Rusticity has become the model for nature, though it is no longer reflective even of rural life.

As discussed at the beginning of this chapter, twentieth-century painters have largely abandoned naturalism and have discovered perception anew. In an important sense, landscape architects have lagged behind these artistic developments and have transferred to actual landscapes around us the very conventions the painters have abandoned. As a result, typical spectators of the landscape have become complacent and comfortable with a sentimental version of the pastoral dream.

Contemporary Art
and Environmental Design

The forces of nature and society are indeed about us. Drought, acid rain, loss of ozone, pesticides in our food, and syringes washing up on beaches remind us that our society threatens the landscape we daily face. More than ever, we may desire the pastoral illusion, but no number of pleasant scenes or beautiful views can disguise our dependence on the resources provided by nature and the city. Tityrus is no longer sufficient; perhaps he never was. Today we need Meliboeus, with his commitment to destabilizing the conventions that have been so comforting. We need a new image of nature, one that supplants the pictorial view that has for so many centuries illustrated (but only partially) Virgil's *Eclogues*.

The craggy river valley or mountain top that so invigorated eighteenth-century landscape enthusiasts is not the answer. Nor is the answer the "wild" and democratic park promulgated by nineteenth-century America, in which one contemplated nature in splendid isolation. Nor is it the lavishly designed, touristic, consumer attraction of the twentieth century. These environments, which package recreation, have become stale to our senses and do not help us to reactivate our numbed environmental responses.

How can contemporary environmental designers recruit Meliboeus to bring tension to design? Should we illustrate to spectators that we are radically modifying the environment that exists outside the pastoral illusion? Should we fill the pleasant meadow with syringes to show that what exists outside its borders must eventually encroach upon it? How do we begin? Where do we look for this nature? Where is Meliboeus when we need him?

There is much to be done. I propose that, as has so often happened in the past, contemporary art can perhaps supply the inspiration needed to invigorate environmental design. In what follows, I shall briefly discuss several artists who have left the museums and galleries to make art in the landscape. Perhaps it is to such artists that landscape architecture can turn.

———

Robert Smithson's earthworks reject the idea that nature is soft, serpentine, and forested. *Asphalt Rundown* (1969), located outside Rome, is a site that had been industrially exploited and abandoned. Needless to say, it is far removed from our typical view of nature. Smithson argued that "we have to develop a different sense of nature . . . that includes [culture]. . . . As an artist it is sort of interesting to take on the persona of a geologic agent where [culture] actually becomes part of the process rather than overcoming it."[6] A work such as *Asphalt Rundown* can only be understood as an attempt to reinterpret pictorial conventions in order to expand our view of the landscape.[7]

James Turrell is an environmental sculptor whose materials are space and light. He is spending a lifetime working on Roden Crater in Arizona, transforming it into a space that will leave a powerful impression on its spectators. According to Suzi Gablik, "Central to Turrell's conception is the notion that art is experiential and spiritual rather than stylistic and aesthetic. Since the essence of our culture of estrangement is that we do not see ourselves as part of the natural world—scientific consciousness insists on a rigid distinction between observer and observed—the primary model for our experience of art has followed a similar pattern."[8]

A sculptor such as Mary Miss makes direct use of pictorial techniques. She engages spectators' participation not by exposing a wide panorama but by causing the spectators to look through one object to the next in order to gain a false perspective. She creates very specific views composed of vertically layered space, in overlaid screens framing shifting perspectives that unfold sequentially and yet are never fully revealed. As a result, what might have passed unnoticed or been diffused instead becomes memorable and distinct.

Robert Irwin began as a painter but has been making sculpture in environments as diverse as forests and the interiors of buildings. His advice to landscape architects suggests that they are not fully realizing nonpictorial, that is, natural, phenomena: "Each landscape architect seems to be inclined to give away his or her most powerful tools: presence, movement, scale, phenomena. . . . They have the varying phenomena of a situation, the change in day to play with, the properties of all that light. And they have scale. . . . You move through space, you participate in the space, you act in the space. To my mind these are elements you absolutely have got to have people involved in. Especially to have them come in not as a shrine or as a special place. The beauty of what happens in the landscape is that you come upon things accidentally. . . . Landscape architects have the power to put all that back in the picture."[9]

Not only have artists such as the four just mentioned worked right in the landscape, but several are actually returning to landscape painting. They are doing so, however, precisely in order to challenge the pictorialization of nature. While these painters of course depend on an understanding of the naturalistic tradition, they have manipulated the conventional view in order to represent our visual and environmental experience; they borrow bits of images from places we recognize and from historical landscape paintings. They splice these together, mutilate parts, present fractures and warped glimpses. Rather than looking at landscapes themselves or "contemplating nature," these artists depend on familiar pictures as sources because they understand how powerful images have been in our perception of landscape and nature.

In "Unnatural Landscapes," Mary Ellen Haus describes several landscape painters who question the pictorialization of nature: "Landscape painting is no longer just a picture window, a nature portrait with the artist as faithful recorder. Created by artists who live and work in the city, this new landscape gives us nature at second hand— almost as memory—using twice-removed images that have turned landscape into a readymade. The landscape-painting tradition, not the natural world, is the given for these artists. And they, in turn, approach landscape not to transcribe but to transform."[10]

Sensational, yet strangely familiar, landscape features are central to landscape paintings by Michael Zwack, one of the painters discussed by Haus. Where have we seen them before? The apparent familiarity of Zwack's paintings is based on our familiarity not with places but with pictures—images that have been pirated from sources such as nature and travel magazines, which are dependent upon the historical conventions for creating a view. These are the images that have been used to sell places. Zwack transforms—and redeems—these land-scapes by destroying their touristic images.

Mark Innerst also engages us with the promise of the familiar. In his paintings, the familiarity comes from glimpses of nineteenth-century American luminists—for example, paintings by John Frederick Kensett (see fig. 10.2)—which Innerst resurrects, remakes, and then reverently places in antique frames. "But once he conjures up an age of innocence, Innerst shifts it into the age of experience. Beneath the paintings' restraint and exquisitely imitated nineteenth-century qualities, their cores seethe with irony. . . . His art works two extremes at once. As he says it, 'It's a picnic area or it's the apocalypse.'"[11]

Joan Nelson renders delicate expanses of moors and tundras (which recall Whistler and seventeenth-century Dutch panoramas) in layers of oil paint and wax on thick board. "The milky, greasy surfaces seem to embalm her imagery, which she has lifted from art-history books and recomposed. While they strongly evoke their primary sources—the Northern landscapes of Altdorfer, the Ruisdaels, and van Goyen—Nelson has stripped the originals of their essence, their crispness and detail. She scores and nicks her paintings' surfaces to produce a disturbing filter that looks as if it were the result of centuries of wear."[12] Indeed, the familiar compositional conventions are worn, and Nelson, by defacing them, illustrates the spectator's resistance to admitting that they no longer evoke responses. "For Nelson, who shares the current skepticism toward the possibility of originality, there could scarcely be a better means to challenge art's status than to tamper with a convention that is the essence of beauty, freshness, tradition—landscape."[13]

Tom Brazelton also tampers with the conventions of landscape painting. He literally stains the vaporous atmospheres he creates with paint and then traps them behind a polyurethane veneer. His looming, skylike images are perceptions of nature and of landscape painting. They vividly evoke sensations of movement, light, shadow, and atmosphere. Brazelton's earliest landscapes were deliberate clichés that epitomized the paintings he saw in restaurants and homes while growing up in the Middle West in the early 1960s. He is working with the dynamics of desire and fulfillment. His atmospheric forms, while presenting an attractive landscape image, are trapped and out of reach. Retreating empty-handed, spectators are left with only their own reflections on the hard and shining surfaces.

Dike Blair also avoids the sentimental pastoral. Instead, he tries to rejoin nature and culture. His landscapes are places where a moon, sun, or earth readily jumps from its orbit to become a billiard ball, a fluorescent light, or the AT&T logo; a cocktail is toppled over a painted Kensett seascape; a moonlit body of water is pasted next to a photograph of an extraordinarily orange sunset inscribed by utility poles. And the impression these images offer is an oddly alluring hybrid. Blair's compositions recognize the frenzied encounters we now have with landscapes in which the nineteenth-century American transcendentalists once immersed themselves. Blair, however, is not emphasizing the unnaturalness of the union of nature and culture; he is expressing its beauty.

In a 1989 exhibition, "Landscape Re-Viewed: Contemporary Reflections on a Traditional Theme," at the Walker Art Center in Minneapolis, Innerst, Nelson, and four other landscape painters whose works were exhibited there illustrated their dependence on and manipulation of traditional landscape conventions. Mary Jo Vath reflected upon the traditional portrait convention of placing a sitter before a landscape. (See, e.g., fig. 6.3.) Her *Mirror* features the background landscape from Leonardo's *Mona Lisa*. But in place of the woman who has come to represent the epitome of mysterious feminine beauty, a mirror faces the spectator. In other paintings, Vath has replaced the human sitter with grotesque counterparts that seem either to mock the vanity of the sitter or to question the authority of those who sit elevated above the landscape. Projected into outer space, the spectator of Vath's *Black Globe* sees the earth as the NASA sphere familiar to us in full-page advertisements. In fact, seeing the earth as the distant sphere in NASA photographs is the ultimate illustration of the pictorialization of nature.[14]

Donald Suggs's large, abstract patterns echo the colors of the landscapes behind them. These abstractions underscore the fact that we are looking not at nature but at a painting of nature. Nelsen Valentine also reaffirms the artificiality of his images. Painted in clear varnish, superimposed patterns appear and disappear as we move past each work, heightening our awareness of the surface of the painting.

"By underscoring the nature of these paintings as objects, the artists psychologically push us away from their images at the same time as they invite us into the work through the use of illusionistic space, intimate proportions, and glossy seductive surfaces. This is not, however, simply a gratuitous game of seduction-and-rejection on the part of the artists. In our commercialized culture, pictured landscapes are used to sell a wide variety of commodities and ideas—from beer and cars to sophistication and national pride. With this in mind, these artists work to reinforce our awareness of the artificiality of their images, reminding us that, in the end, we are just looking at pictures and that pictures can be used for different purposes. Vath's painting of a set of fishing lures dangling before a landscape symbolizes the game of simultaneous gratification and frustration of desires that is afoot: the landscape can 'hook' us if we let our attraction to the image overwhelm our awareness of the way it is being used."[15] Finally, although it may be only pictures that we are looking at, these pictures tell us that they have a powerful influence on our perception of the landscape.

Throughout this book, I have maintained that the goal of naturalistic landscape painting is to convince the spectator that a believable view of the world can be pictured as if through a window. Because these contemporary painters make representational works and refer to historical landscape paintings, it may seem that they too are naturalists. But they are not. By a variety of means, these artists force upon us a sense of self-consciousness that denies us the ability to transport ourselves imaginatively into the depicted scene. They have done so by challenging the conventions, and thereby the presuppositions, of the scenic view. They have abandoned naturalism. These are landscapes that recognize conflict. These artists have consulted Meliboeus.

———

In the nineteenth century, America's self-image was shaped largely through an unmodified conception of wilderness mediated by a picture of beauty inherited from Europe. Contrary to the naturalistic tradition of painting which culminated with pictures of the American wilderness, recent American painters have abandoned the pretense that what is enclosed in the frame represents nature. Instead, what is enclosed brings to mind a lengthy history of references to nature placed alongside, or superimposed upon, selected evidence of how that American wilderness has been modified and transformed into landscape. These pictures teach us that nature is not simply something green and pretty.

I trust that by now the reader has noticed that unlike every other chapter of this book, this one contains few pictures to document it. This is no accident. Instead it is a deliberate attempt to offer a challenge to the reader: look for yourself at contemporary landscape paintings and photographs, sculpture, and environmental art. These works ask us to question the conflicts inherent in our attitude toward nature, as well as the role of painting in creating "the view." Go and look for landscapes that fit the compositional conventions of the scenic view, and compare them to the majority that do not. Investigate places for their potential to tell us about ourselves. Scenic spots can no longer be understood as providing a picture of nature. That the landscape is a cultural construction can best be seen by taking a critical look at ordinary and spectacular places, and bearing in mind the history of how the landscape has been pictured.

Notes

1. Introduction:
The Nature of Landscape

1. Pollan discusses the history of roses in his book *Second Nature*. (Full bibliographic information for the works cited in the notes can be found in the Bibliography.)
2. Lewis, 45–46.
3. For fascinating reading on the subject of woman as nature, see Griffin; Merchant; Fabricant, "Binding and Dressing Nature's Loose Tresses"; and Paglia.
4. Fabricant, "Binding and Dressing Nature's Loose Tresses," 110.
5. Shepard, entry for April 28, 1857.
6. Quoted in Nash, 126.
7. Marsh, 10–11.
8. Clark, 238.
9. Nash, 83.
10. Gombrich, *Norm and Form*, 118.
11. Jackson, *Vernacular Landscape*, 8. Italics added.
12. Ibid., 6.
13. Ibid., 12.
14. Barrell, *Idea of Landscape*, 1.
15. Leach, *Rhetoric of Space*, 41, for example, defines naturalism as that which "procures an empirical illusion of spatial recession through the diminution of background figures, and the attenuation of background colors."
16. Gombrich, *Story of Art*, 34.
17. Crandell, "In Capability."
18. *Compact Oxford English Dictionary*, s.v. "landscape."
19. Many twentieth-century scholars discuss the importance of seventeenth-century landscape painting to the development of the eighteenth-century English landscape garden. This scholarship begins with Elizabeth Manwaring's 1925 book entitled *Italian Landscape in Eighteenth Century England*.
20. Clark, 1.
21. Hartt, 68.
22. Gombrich, *Norm and Form*, 116.
23. Ibid., 117.

2. *Confronting the Spectator:*
The Ancient World

1. My intention here, as elsewhere, is not so much to present a comprehensive historical analysis of landscape architecture or landscape painting as it is to isolate and to comment on those trends and themes I have discussed in chapter 1.

2. This chapter is heavily reliant on the work of Vincent Scully; here and in the remainder of the chapter, numbers appearing in parentheses are citations of page numbers in his book *The Earth, the Temple, and the Gods.*

   It should be noted here that there has been some controversy about Scully's hypotheses. In a review published in the *Art Bulletin*, Homer A. Thompson concluded that "the hypothesis advanced by Scully, if confirmed, would raise a serious paradox in our interpretation of the ancient attitude toward nature. If Scully is right, we must assume that in one branch of architecture very great importance was attached by the Greeks to the natural setting of man's activities at a time when the same subject was receiving only the most summary attention from Greek writers, sculptors, and painters." In Scully's preface to the 1969 edition of his book he responded by saying, "Still, a serious problem of method apparently exists here for those classical archaeologists who were trained to catalogue data according to positivistic criteria based upon a contemporary or, more likely, a nineteenth-century model of reality. Landscape shapes, for example, simply do not exist for them artistically in other than picturesque terms." The *Book Review Digest* in 1970 stated, "The first edition of this book [*The Earth, the Temple, and the Gods*] made the experts uneasy; it attempted answers to a kind of question they (classical archaeologists, historians, philologists) had not themselves formulated, let alone answered. . . . There has been controversy . . . but it is unlikely that emergent official truth will succeed in ignoring Scully's work. Students need access to the book if only to understand the controversy."

3. He does this in the following way: each chapter is devoted to a specific god or goddess, and discusses site-specific and god-specific relationships.

4. Zucker, 29.

5. For a study of the symbols and images of the goddess in the art and religion of the Neolithic period and in the civilizations of the Near East and Crete, Scully recommends G. R. Levy's *Gate of the Horn.*

6. See Scully, figs. 263–74, for plan views and photographs.

7. Zucker, 33.

8. It is interesting to consider a contemporary, albeit quite simple, example to illustrate an important point about space-positive design. When porches fail to provide space-positive design, they tend to degenerate. Consider porches on older houses in America. These houses typically were close to the sidewalk and the street, where the activity of a neighborhood was mainly found, and the porches provided a social transition between private space (the interior), and public space (the street). Particularly in good weather, conversation could begin right in the space between the porch and the sidewalk.

By contrast, today's suburban houses are set deeply back from the street and are no longer space-positive. They no longer provide a transition space between interior and exterior. Consequently, porches have degenerated into concrete pads with no place to sit. Who would want to? A person sitting on the porch would be too far from the street to initiate a conversation with anyone. Moreover, many suburban developments have no sidewalks, and the streets are just for cars. When porches (e.g., the concrete pads of today's suburbs) are no longer space positive, they contribute to a more frontal and pictorial, less social, and more status-oriented presentation of the facade to the public street, and become good places for foundation plantings.

3. Staging the Spectacle:
Hellenistic and Roman Times

1. Scully, 192–93.
2. Ibid., 193.
3. Kernodle, 2.
4. Ibid., 20.
5. Vitruvius, 151.
6. Ibid., 211.
7. Ibid.
8. Here and throughout the text of this chapter, numbers in parentheses are citations of page numbers in Leach, *Rhetoric of Space.*
9. Homer, 154–55, Lattimore's translation.
10. Pearsall and Salter, 7. "There is the strong possibility that landscapes such as these may have been inspired by pictures. . . . There is a temptation to see close connections between Virgil's epic landscapes and the epic narrative painting fashionable in his day, such as the *Odyssey Landscapes,* four of which portray the arrival of Odysseus in the land of the Laestrygonians."
11. Cafritz, Gowing, and Rosand, 26.
12. Olmsted, 46.
13. Stilgoe, *Common Landscape,* 3, distinguishes "landscape" from "cityscape."
14. The quotations from Virgil that follow are from the translation by Rieu in Virgil, *The Pastoral Poems,* 19–27. This eclogue was chosen largely because of Leo Marx's discussion of it in *Machine in the Garden.*
15. Leach, *Vergil,* 116–17.
16. Ibid., 133.
17. Ibid., 136.
18. Marx, *Machine in the Garden,* 25.

4. Cloistering the Spectator:
The Middle Ages

1. Clark, 3.
2. Ibid.

3. Pearsall and Salter, 30.
4. Ibid., 26. "One might say further that it is when cities again begin to assume prime importance, detaching themselves from the rural environment and subduing it to their own concerns, that the pastoral begins to reappear."
5. Ibid., 27–28.
6. Ibid., 30.
7. Ibid.
8. Panofsky, "Perspective as Symbolic Form," 8. A new translation of this work has recently been published.
9. Pearsall and Salter, 38–39.
10. Panofsky, "Perspective as Symbolic Form," 10.
11. Song of Sol. 4:12, quoted in Edgerton, 123.

5. Centering the Spectator: The Renaissance

1. The Annunciation comprises a series of moments, ranging in number from three to seven. E.g., Baxandall, *Painting and Experience,* 51–56, refers to five moments: Disquiet, Reflection, Inquiry, Submission, and Merit.
2. Although there are examples of landscape painting in the Hellenistic period (e.g., the Odyssey Landscapes) as well as examples of landscapes in medieval illuminations, landscape itself was not considered a primary subject of painting in the West until the seventeenth century, and that development was dependent on the tools of linear perspective.
3. Hartt, 70.
4. Panofsky, "Perspective as Symbolic Form," 12.
5. Ibid., 13.
6. Ibid., 14.
7. According to Baxandall, *Painting and Experience,* 15, the diminishing use of gold and ultramarine was the result of "very complex and discrete sources—a frightening social mobility with its problem of dissociating oneself from the flashy new rich; the acute physical shortage of gold in the fifteenth century."
8. Cardile, 192.
9. Ibid., 193.
10. Battisti, 14.
11. Ibid., 11.
12. Ibid., 25–26.
13. Adams, 68.

6. Elevating the Spectator: The Renaissance

1. *Compact Oxford English Dictionary,* s.v. "panorama."
2. Quoted in Clark, 10.
3. Ibid.

4. Gould, 5.
5. Pearsall and Salter, 182.
6. The painting *The Good Government of the City* is adjacent to, and to the left of, *The Good Government of the Country.*
7. Gombrich, *Story of Art,* 161.
8. Hartt, 289–90.
9. Gombrich, *Story of Art,* 180.

7. Bewildering the Spectator:
The Northern Renaissance

1. Gombrich, *Norm and Form,* 109.
2. Cosgrove and Daniels, 254.
3. Cafritz, Gowing, and Rosand, 26. "Throughout the postclassical world the pastoral tradition continued to be a source of poetic inspiration. It found new life in the Renaissance, especially with the publication in the opening years of the sixteenth century of Jacopo Sannazaro's *Arcadia,* written in Italian and therefore accessible to a large audience."
4. Clark, 115, accepts Wind's arguments in *Giorgione's Tempesta* as authoritative. The reader might wish to refer to Leo Marx's discussion of Shakespeare's *Tempest* as an American pastoral fable in *Machine in the Garden,* 34–72.
5. Wind, 3.
6. Clark, 115.
7. Nash, 1.
8. Gombrich, *Norm and Form,* 116.
9. Clark, 75.
10. Ibid., 78.
11. Sorte. The treatise, "Osservazioni nella pittura," has been republished in a modern compilation.
12. Gombrich, *Norm and Form,* 118.
13. Clark, 56.
14. Aristotle, *Poetics,* 4.2–4, translation by David Roochnik, personal communication.

8. Landscape Prospects:
The Seventeenth Century

1. Robert Boyle first constructed a box camera with a lens for viewing landscapes. *Encyclopaedia Brittanica,* s.v. "camera obscura," 4:658–60.
2. Manwaring, 13.
3. Ibid., v.
4. Barrell, *Idea of Landscape,* 8.
5. Ibid., 8.
6. Ibid., 11.
7. Clark, 138–39. Italics added.
8. It is particularly important when discussing this moment, the peak of landscape painting, to recognize the theory of prospect and refuge as

developed by Appleton in *Experience of Landscape,* although Appleton's theory applies to general discussions of framing, distancing, and vistas.

9. See Hartman, 317–18.
10. Fry, 226–27.
11. Ibid.
12. Clark, 129.
13. Sunderland, 786.
14. Ibid., 786.
15. Ibid., 785.
16. Manwaring, 229–30.
17. Sunderland, 788.
18. Stilgoe, *Common Landscape,* 24.
19. Barrell, *Idea of Landscape,* 1.
20. Alpers, 37–38.
21. Ibid., 37–38.
22. Ibid., 27.
23. Ibid.
24. Denis Wood, personal communication, 1989.
25. Schama, 67.
26. Ibid., 74.
27. Ibid., 80.
28. Ibid.
29. Ogden, 166.
30. Quoted in Gould, 4.

9. Spectators of the Picturesque: Eighteenth-Century England

1. Hussey, 5.
2. Ibid., 10.
3. Tuan, 121. "Appreciation of scenery is much less common than we think. Almost everywhere, attachment is to homeplace, and the more intense feeling of awe is directed to a sacred locality. In the presence of a home or a sacred place, all one's senses are actively engaged. Distancing—intrinsic to visual and aesthetic appreciation—is absent."
4. Hussey, 84.
5. Quoted in ibid., 24.
6. Quoted in ibid., 88.
7. Fabricant, "Aesthetics and Politics," 64.
8. Hunt and Willis, 12–13.
9. Barrell, *Idea of Landscape,* 5.
10. Quoted in Hunt, "Ut Pictura Poesis," 89.
11. Addison, 148 (originally published in the *Spectator* in 1712, essay no. 413).
12. Ibid., 142 (originally published in the *Spectator* in 1712, essay no. 412).
13. Fabricant, "Aesthetics and Politics," 55.

14. Addison, 151 (originally published in the *Spectator* in 1712, essay no. 414).
15. Hussey, 18.
16. Manwaring, 4.
17. Hussey, 31.
18. From Dyer's "Grongar Hill," quoted in Manwaring, 99.
19. Thacker, *History of Gardens,* 185.
20. Hunt and Willis, 12.
21. Ibid., 189.
22. Although many eighteenth-century writers were talking about the "new" idea of making gardens irregular, which was based on ancient literature and seventeenth-century paintings, Henry Wotton had said as early as 1624 that "gardens should bee irregular." Quoted in Hunt and Willis, 48. As an ambassador to Italy, he was greatly influenced by Italian gardens.
23. Jellicoe and Jellicoe, 235.
24. Hunt and Willis, 15.
25. Ibid.
26. Thacker, *History of Gardens,* 197.
27. Ibid., 194.
28. Quoted in Watkins, 29.
29. Ibid.
30. Pevsner, 100.
31. Hunt, "Ut Pictura Poesis," distinguishes between the landscape garden's connection to painting and literature, which he calls the "academic picturesque," and the garden's retreat from "narrative" in the second half of the century. In the introduction to Hunt and Willis, *Genius of the Place,* the authors outline the development of the landscape garden in the eighteenth century, with particular reference to painting. I have closely followed the arguments presented in these two works.
32. "We know that Kent had in his collection examples of Italian landscape by Salvator and Gaspar, at least." Manwaring, 131. "We know that in later years he himself owned originals or copies of paintings by Claude." Thacker, *History of Gardens,* 186.
33. Quoted in Hussey, 130.
34. The design was inspired by a remarkable essay in the *Spectator* by Joseph Addison on the true nature of honor and virtue. In it, Addison described a dream in which he had found himself walking through a wood behind a group of people carrying the standard of ambition. The essential features of the Elysian Fields are all in Addison's essay: a long straight path terminated by a Temple of Virtue, beyond which, over the river Styx, was a Temple of Honour; nearby is a ruinous Temple of Vanity (Modern Virtue at Stowe, built deliberately and ironically as a ruin). The types of people and also the effigies correspond to the statues actually set up in the gardens at Stowe. Watkin, 18.
35. Hunt, "Ut Pictura Poesis," 92.
36. Ibid.
37. See Robinson for a scholarly discussion of the politics of the picturesque.

38. Barrell, *Idea of Landscape,* 2–3.
39. Quotation from Stroud, 29–30.
40. A garden design that exemplifies Hogarth's theory and precedes Brown's work is West Wycombe. A garden created by its owner, Sir Francis Dasher, it imbibed the eighteenth century's enthusiasm for Claudian landscape by creating "a landscape, a painting, a poem (each term is appropriate) in which, to follow Addison's suggestion of 1712, a man has indeed made 'a pretty Landskip of his own possessions.' " Thacker, *History of Gardens,* 203. It should not be too surprising that Sir Dasher conceived of his possession as having serpentine forms intended to represent women's bodies. The lakes and gardens were "laid out by a curious arrangement of streams, bushes and plantation to represent the female form." Thacker, *History of Gardens,* 204. Indeed, it looks strikingly like our own parks today.
41. Hogarth, 239–40.
42. Ibid.
43. Sunderland, 785.
44. Hunt and Willis, 31.
45. Quoted in Hussey, 139.
46. See Hoskins for a detailed description of the enclosure acts.
47. Bermingham, 13–15.
48. Hunt, "Ut Pictura Poesis," 87.
49. Bermingham, 13–15.
50. Ibid., 14.
51. Hunt and Willis, 318.
52. Ibid., 20.
53. Watkins, vii.
54. Quoted in Smithson, 49.
55. Quoted in Barrell, *Idea of Landscape,* 5.
56. Quoted in Hunt and Willis, 350.
57. Quoted in ibid., 349. The italics appeared in Hunt and Willis.
58. Quoted in Hussey, 70. Italics are mine.
59. Quoted in ibid., 181.
60. Hussey, 192.
61. Ibid., 206.
62. Ibid., 160.
63. For an exciting discussion of visual assessment, see Wood.

10. *Democratic Landscape: Nineteenth-Century America*

1. Harris, 118.
2. Marx, *Machine in the Garden,* 9–10.
3. Ibid.
4. Hollander, 352.
5. Quoted in Nash, 82.
6. Novak, *Nature and Culture,* 173.
7. Ibid., 189.
8. Ibid., 148–49.

9. Ibid., 228–30. Italics added.
10. Ibid., 228–30.
11. Ibid., 10.
12. Quoted in Nash, 100–101.
13. Hollander, 357–58.
14. Novak, *Nature and Culture*, 171.
15. Ibid., 171.
16. Marx, *Machine in the Garden*, 220–21.
17. Novak, *Nature and Culture*, 173–74.
18. I believe this information was published by Neil Harris.
19. Jackson, *Landscapes*, 7.
20. Quoted in Pool, 145.
21. Hughes, 18.

11. *The Spectator's Perception: The Twentieth Century*

1. Giedion, 497.
2. Chave, 119.
3. Berger, *About Looking*, 76.
4. The concept of "attractions" is based on MacCannell.
5. See Mackie's discussion of the pastoral in Roman time: "In the course of the first century A.D., people's faith in the capacity of art to do what nature did, only better, reached what to us seem absurd proportions" (11). Also see Lowenthal: "The contemporary tendency to find beauty and good in the 'natural,' and ugliness or squalor in what man dominates is not only moralistic; it is an aesthetic aberration in the history of landscape taste" (20).
6. See Crandell, "Art," 10–16.
7. Ibid.
8. Gablik, 153. Also see Adcock.
9. *Landscape Architecture Magazine,* 103.
10. Haus, 129.
11. Ibid., 130.
12. Ibid.
13. Ibid.
14. For a discussion of the earth image, see Garb.
15. Boswell, 7.

Bibliography

Adams, William Howard. *The French Garden, 1500–1800*. New York: George Braziller, 1979.

Adcock, Craig. *James Turrell: The Art of Light and Space*. Berkeley: University of California Press, 1990.

Addison, Joseph. *Essays in Criticism and Literary Theory*. Edited by John Loftis. Northbrook, Ill.: AHM Publishing, 1975.

Alberti, Leon Battista. *On Painting*. Westport, Conn.: Greenwood Press, 1976.

Alpers, Svetlana. *The Art of Describing: Dutch Art in the Seventeenth Century*. Chicago: University of Chicago Press, 1983.

Appleton, Jay. *The Experience of Landscape*. New York: John Wiley & Sons, 1975.

Arnheim, Rudolph. "Order and Complexity in Landscape Design." In *Toward a Psychology of Art*, 123–35. Berkeley: University of California Press, 1966.

Barrell, John. *The Dark Side of Landscape: The Rural Poor in English Painting, 1730–1840*. New York: Cambridge University Press, 1980.

———. *The Idea of Landscape and the Sense of Place*. Cambridge: Cambridge University Press, 1972.

———. *Political Theory of Painting from Reynolds to Hazlitt*. New Haven: Yale University Press, 1986.

Battisti, Eugenio. "Natura Artificiosa to Natura Artificialis." In *The Italian Garden*, edited by David R. Coffin, 1–36. Washington, D.C.: Dumbarton Oaks, 1972.

Baxandall, Michael. *Patterns of Intention: On the Historical Explanation of Pictures*. New Haven: Yale University Press, 1985.

———. *Painting and Experience in Fifteenth Century Italy: A Primer in the Social History of Pictorial Style*. Oxford: Clarendon Press, 1972.

Berger, John. *About Looking*. London: Writers & Readers, 1980.

———. *Ways of Seeing*. London: British Broadcasting Company and Penguin Books, 1972.

Bermingham, Ann. *Landscape and Ideology: The English Rustic Tradition, 1740–1850*. Berkeley: University of California Press, 1986.

Book Review Digest. Review of *The Earth, the Temple, and the Gods: Greek Sacred Architecture*, by Vincent Scully. (1970): 1263.

Boswell, Peter. *Viewpoints: Landscape Re-Viewed: Contemporary Reflections on a Traditional Theme*. Minneapolis, Minn: Walker Art Center, 1989.

Burke, Edmund. *A Philosophical Enquiry into the Origin of Our Ideas of the Sublime and Beautiful*. Edited by James T. Boulton. London: University of Notre Dame Press, 1968.

Cafritz, Robert, Lawrence Gowing, and David Rosand. *Places of Delight: The Pastoral Landscape.* Washington, D.C.: Philips Collection, 1986.

Cardile, Paul J. "Observations on the Iconography of Leonardo da Vinci's Uffizi *Annunication.*" *Studies in Iconography* 7–8 (1981–82): 189–208.

Carli, Enzo. *The Landscape in Art.* New York: William Morrow & Co., 1980.

Chave, Anna C. "O'Keeffe and the Masculine Gaze." *Art in America* 78, no. 1 (1990): 115–24.

Clark, Kenneth. *Landscape into Art.* New York: Harper & Row, 1976.

Comito, Terry. *The Idea of the Garden in the Renaissance.* New Brunswick, N.J.: Rutgers University Press, 1978.

The Compact Edition of the Oxford English Dictionary. Vol. 2. Oxford: Oxford University Press, 1971.

Coniff, Gregory. *Common Ground.* New Haven: Yale University Press, 1985.

Cornish, Vaughn. *Scenery and the Sense of Sight.* Cambridge: Cambridge University Press, 1935.

Cosgrove, Denis. *Social Formation and Symbolic Landscape.* London: Croom Helm, 1984.

Cosgrove, Denis, and Stephen Daniels, eds. *The Iconography of Landscape.* Cambridge: Cambridge University Press, 1988.

Crandell, Gina. "When Art Challenges Beauty." *Landscape* 29, no. 1 (1986): 10–16.

———. "In Capability: From Blenheim to General Foods." *Landscape Architecture Magazine* 74, no. 3 (1984): 48–53.

Czestochowski, Joseph S. *The American Landscape Tradition.* New York: E. P. Dutton, 1982.

Dubos, René. *The Wooing of Earth.* New York: Charles Scribner's Sons, 1980.

Egerton, Samuel Y., Jr. "Mensurare Temporalia Facit Geometria Spiritualis: Some Fifteenth-Century Notions about When and Where the Annunciation Happened." In *Studies in Late Medieval and Renaissance Painting in Honor of Millard Meiss,* 115–30. New York: New York University Press, 1977.

Encyclopaedia Brittanica, 1958.

Fabricant, Carole. "The Aesthetics and Politics of Landscape in the Eighteenth Century." In *Studies in Eighteenth-Century British Art and Aesthetics,* edited by R. Cohen, 49–81. Berkeley: University of California Press, 1985.

———. "Binding and Dressing Nature's Tresses: The Ideology of Augustan Landscape Design." *Eighteenth-Century Studies* (1979): 109–35.

Flexner, James Thomas. *That Wilder Image.* Boston: Little, Brown, & Co., 1962.

Fry, Roger. *Vision and Design.* New York: Brentano's, 1924.

Gablik, Suzi. "Dream Space." *Art in America* 75 (March 1987): 132–33, 153.

Garb, Yaakov Jerome. "Perspective or Escape: Ecofeminist Musings on Contemporary Earth Images." In *Reweaving the World: The Emergence of Ecofeminism,* edited and with essays by Irene Diamond and Gloria Feman Orenstein. San Francisco, Calif.: Sierra Club Books, 1990.

Gardner, Helen. *Art through the Ages.* 7th ed. New York: Harcourt Brace Jovanovich, 1980.

Gibson, James J. *The Senses Considered as Perceptual Systems.* Boston: Houghton Mifflin Co., 1966.

Giedion, Sigfried. *Space, Time, and Architecture.* 5th ed. Cambridge, Mass.: Harvard University Press, 1967.

Gombrich, E. H. *Norm and Form: Studies in the Art of the Renaissance.* London: Phaidon Press, 1966.

————. *Art and Illusion: A Study in the Psychology of Pictorial Representation.* Washington, D.C.: Pantheon Books, 1960.

————. *The Story of Art.* Oxford: Phaidon Press, 1950.

Gould, Cecil. *Space in Landscape.* London: National Gallery, 1974.

Griffin, Susan. *Woman and Nature: The Roaring Inside Her.* New York: Harper & Row, 1978.

Harris, Neil. *The Artist in American Society: The Formative Years, 1790–1860.* New York: George Braziller, 1966.

Hartman, Geoffrey H. *Beyond Formalism.* New Haven: Yale University Press, 1970.

Hartt, Frederick. *History of the Italian Renaissance,* 2d ed. New York: Harry Abrams, 1979.

Haus, Mary Ellen. "The Unnatural Landscape." *ARTnews* 87, no. 1 (1988): 128–132.

Helphand, Kenneth I. "Landscape Films." *Landscape Journal* 5, no. 1 (1986): 1–8.

Hess, Thomas B., and John Ashbery, eds. *Light in Art.* New York: Collier Books, 1969.

Hipple, Walter J., Jr. *The Beautiful, the Sublime, and the Picturesque in Eighteenth-Century British Aesthetic Theory.* Carbondale: Southern Illinois University Press, 1957.

Hockney, David. *Cameraworks.* New York: Alfred A. Knopf, 1984.

Hogarth, William. *The Analysis of Beauty.* 1753. Reprint. Pittsfield, Mass.: Silver Lotus Shop, 1909.

Hollander, Anne. *Moving Pictures.* New York: Alfred A. Knopf, 1988.

Homer. *The Odyssey of Homer.* Translated with an introduction by Richmond Lattimore. New York: Harper & Row, 1965.

Hoskins, W. G. *The Making of the English Landscape.* London: Hodder & Stoughton, 1955.

Hughes, Robert. *The Shock of the New.* New York: Alfred A. Knopf, 1981.

Hunt, John Dixon. *The Figure in the Landscape: Poetry, Painting, and Gardening during the Eighteenth Century.* Baltimore: Johns Hopkins University Press, 1976.

————. "Ut Pictura Poesis, Ut Pictura Hortus, and the Picturesque." *Word and Image* 1, no. 1 (1985): 87–111.

Hunt, John Dixon, and Peter Willis, eds. *The Genius of the Place: The English Landscape Garden, 1620–1820.* London: Paul Elek, 1975.

Hussey, Christopher. *The Picturesque: Studies in a Point of View.* London: Cass, 1967.

Jackson, John Brinckerhoff. *Discovering the Vernacular Landscape.* New Haven: Yale University Press, 1984.

————. *Landscapes*. Edited by Ervin H. Zube. Amherst: University of Massachusetts Press, 1970.

————. *The Necessity for Ruins*. Amherst: University of Massachusetts Press, 1980.

Jeffares, Bo. *Landscape Painting*. Oxford: Phaidon Press, 1979.

Jellicoe, G. A. *Studies in Landscape Design*. Vol. 3. London: Oxford University Press, 1970.

Jellicoe, Geoffrey, and Susan Jellicoe. *The Landscape of Man*. London: Thames & Hudson, 1975.

Kernodle, George R. *From Art to Theatre: Form and Convention in the Renaissance*. Chicago: University of Chicago Press, 1944.

Knight, Richard Payne. *An Analytical Inquiry into the Principles of Taste*. 4th ed. London: T. Payne, 1808.

————. *The Landscape: A Didactic Poem in Three Books*. London, 1794.

Kolodny, Annette. *The Lay of the Land*. Chapel Hill: University of North Carolina Press, 1975.

Landscape Architecture Magazine. "Comments from the Juries." 78, no. 7 (1988): 99–103.

Lang, S. "The Genesis of the English Landscape Garden." In *The Picturesque Garden and Its Influence Outside the British Isles*. Washington, D.C.: Dumbarton Oaks, 1974.

Lawson-Peebles, Robert. Introduction to "The Pastoral Issue" (special issue). *Landscape Research Group Ltd*. 14, no. 1 (1989): 1–3.

Leach, Eleanor Winsor. *The Rhetoric of Space: Literary and Artistic Representations of Landscape in Republican and Augustan Rome*. Princeton: Princeton University Press, 1988.

————. *Vergil's Eclogues: Landscapes of Experience*. Princeton: Princeton University Press, 1974.

Levy, G. R. *The Gate of the Horn: A Study of the Religious Conceptions of the Stone Age, and Their Influence upon European Thought*. New York: Book Collectors Society, 1948.

Lewis, C. S. *Studies in Words*. Cambridge: Cambridge University Press, 1960.

Lowenthal, David. "Not Every Prospect Pleases: What Is Our Criterion for Scenic Beauty?" *Landscape* 12, no. 2 (1962): 19–23.

MacCannell, Dean. *The Tourist: A New Theory of the Leisure Class*. New York: Schocken, 1975.

Machor, James L. *Pastoral Cities: Urban Ideals and the Symbolic Landscape of America*. Madison: University of Wisconsin Press, 1987.

Mackie, Nicola. "Urbanity in a Roman Landscape: The Eclogues of Calpurinus Siculus." *Landscape Research Group Ltd*. 14, no. 1 (1989): 9–14.

McShine, Kynaston, ed. *The Natural Paradise: Painting in America, 1800–1950*. New York: Museum of Modern Art, 1976.

Manwaring, Elizabeth Wheeler. *Italian Landscape in Eighteenth Century England: A Study Chiefly of the Influence of Claude Lorrain and Salvator Rosa on English Taste, 1700–1800*. New York: Oxford University Press, 1925.

Marsh, George Perkins. *Man and Nature*. Edited by David Lowenthal. Cambridge, Mass.: Belknap Press of Harvard University Press, 1965.

Marx, Leo. *The Machine in the Garden: Technology and the Pastoral Ideal in America*. New York: Oxford University Press, 1964.

———. "Pastoralism in America." In *Ideology and Classic American Literature*, edited by Sacvan Bercovitch and Myra Jehlen. Cambridge: Cambridge University Press, 1986.

Meinig, D. W., ed. *The Interpretation of Ordinary Landscapes*. New York: Oxford University Press, 1979.

Merchant, Carolyn. *The Death of Nature: Women, Ecology, and the Scientific Revolution*. San Francisco: Harper & Row, 1980.

Nash, Roderick. *Wilderness and the American Mind*. Rev. ed. New Haven: Yale University Press, 1973.

Nicolson, Marjorie Hope. *Mountain Gloom and Mountain Glory: The Development of the Aesthetics of the Infinite*. Ithaca, N.Y.: Cornell University Press, 1959.

Novak, Barbara. *Nature and Culture: American Landscape and Painting, 1825–1875*. New York: Oxford University Press, 1980.

———. *American Painting of the Nineteenth Century*. New York: Praeger, 1969.

Ogden, H. V. S. *English Taste in Landscape in the Seventeenth Century*. Ann Arbor: University of Michigan Press, 1955.

Olmsted, Frederick Law, Sr. *Forty Years of Landscape Architecture: Central Park*. Edited by Frederick Law Olmsted, Jr., and Theodora Kimball. Cambridge, Mass.: MIT Press, 1973.

Paglia, Camille. *Sexual Personae: Art and Decadence from Nefertiti to Emily Dickinson*. New Haven: Yale University Press, 1991.

Panofsky, Erwin. "Perspective as Symbolic Form." Translated from *Vortrage der Bibliothek Warburg*, 1924–25. Typescript consulted at Parks Library, Iowa State University, Ames, Iowa.

———. *Perspective as Symbolic Form*. Edited by Sanford Clinter and translated by Christopher S. Wood. n.p.: Zone Books, 1991.

Pearsall, Derek, and Elizabeth Salter. *Landscapes and Seasons of the Medieval World*. London: Elek Books, 1973.

Pevsner, Nikolaus. *Studies in Art, Architecture, and Design*. New York: Walker & Company, 1968.

Pollan, Michael. *Second Nature: A Gardener's Education*. New York: Atlantic Monthly Press, 1991.

Pool, Phoebe. *Impressionism*. New York: Oxford University Press. 1979.

Price, Uvedale. *Sir Uvedale Price on the Picturesque*. Compiled by Thomas Dick Lauder. London: Wm. S. Orr & Co., 1842.

Repton, Humphrey. *The Red Books of Humphrey Repton*. Compiled by Edward Malins. London: Basilisk Press, 1976.

Robinson, Sidney K. *Inquiry into the Picturesque*. Chicago: University of Chicago Press, 1991.

Schama, Simon. "Dutch Landscapes: Culture as Foreground." In *Masters of Seventeenth-Century Dutch Landscape Painting*, edited by Peter C. Sutton. Boston: Museum of Fine Arts, 1987.

Scully, Vincent. *The Earth, the Temple, and the Gods: Greek Sacred Architecture*. New Haven: Yale University Press, 1962.

Shepard, Odell, ed. *The Heart of Thoreau's Journals*. New York: Dover Publications, 1961.

Smithson, Robert. *The Writings of Robert Smithson: Essays with Illustrations.* Edited by Nancy Holt. New York: New York University Press, 1979.

Sontag, Susan. *On Photography.* New York: Delta, 1973.

Sorte, Cristoforo. "Osservazione nella pittura." In *Trattati d'arte del cinquecento,* edited by P. Barocchi. Bari, Italy: Scrittori d'Italia, 1960.

Stilgoe, John. "Popular Photography, Scenery Values, and Visual Assessment." *Landscape Journal* 3 (Fall 1984): 111–22.

————. *Common Landscape of America, 1580–1845.* New Haven: Yale University Press, 1982.

Streatfield, David C. "Art and Nature in the English Landscape Garden: Design Theory and Practice, 1700–1818." In *Landscape in the Gardens and the Literature,* edited by Donald M. Roberts. Los Angeles: William Andrews Clark Memorial Library, 1981.

Stroud, Dorothy. *Capability Brown.* London: Faber, 1975.

Sunderland, John. "The Legend and Influence of Salvator Rosa in England in the Eighteenth Century." *Burlington Magazine* 849 (1973): 785–89.

Thacker, Christopher. *The Wildness Pleases: The Origins of Romanticism.* New York: Saint Martin's Press, 1983.

————. *History of Gardens.* London: Croom Helm, 1979.

Thompson, Homer A. Review of *The Earth, the Temple, and the Gods: Greek Sacred Architecture,* by Vincent Scully. *Art Bulletin* 45, no. 3 (1963): 277–80.

Tuan, Yi-Fu. *Segmented Worlds and Self.* Minneapolis: University of Minnesota Press, 1982.

Turner, A. Richard. *The Vision of Landscape in Renaissance Italy.* Princeton: Princeton University Press, 1966.

Turner, Roger. *Capability Brown and the Eighteenth Century English Landscape.* London: Weidenfeld & Nicolson, 1985.

Vasari, Giorgio. *The Essential Vasari: Biographies of the Most Eminent Architects, Painters, and Sculptors of Italy.* Abridged and edited by Betty Burroughs. London: Urwin Books, 1962.

Virgil. *The Pastoral Poems.* Translated by E. V. Rieu. Baltimore: Penguin Books, 1954.

Vitruvius. *Ten Books of Architecture.* Translated by Morris Hicky Morgan. New York: Dover Publications, 1960.

Wartofsky, Marx W. "Picturing and Representing." In *Perception and Pictorial Representation,* edited by Calvin Nodine. New York: Praeger, 1979.

Watkin, David. *The English Vision: The Picturesque in Architecture, Landscape, and Urban Design.* London: John Murray, 1982.

White, John. *The Birth and Rebirth of Pictorial Space.* Boston: Boston Book & Art Shop, 1967.

Wind, Edgar. *Giorgione's Tempesta.* Oxford: Clarendon Press, 1969.

Wood, Denis. "Unnatural Illusions: Some Words about Visual Resource Management." *Landscape Journal* 1 (1988): 192–207.

Zucker, Paul. *Town and Square: From the Agora to the Village Green.* New York: Columbia University Press, 1959.

Index

Designed by Laury A. Egan

Set in Sabon by Brushwood Graphics

Printed on 70-lb. Glatfelter Smooth Eggshell

Bound in Holliston Roxite by The Maple Press Company